JAZZ:
HOT AND HYBRID

WINTHROP SARGEANT

JAZZ:
HOT AND HYBRID

Third Edition, Enlarged

A DA CAPO PAPERBACK

Library of Congress Cataloging in Publication Data

Sargeant, Winthrop, 1903-
Jazz, hot and hybrid.

Bibliography: p.
Includes index.
1. Jazz music. I. Title.
ML3561.J3S3 1975   785.4'2   74-20823
ISBN 0-306-70656-3
ISBN 0-306-80001-2 pbk.

COPYRIGHTS AND ACKNOWLEDGMENTS

ACKNOWLEDGMENTS for the extended examples of music used in this book are made to Mr. Arthur Schwartz for permission to quote from *Dancing In the Dark*, © 1931 by Harms, Inc., to Mr. Jerome Kern to quote from *Who*, © 1925 by T. B. Harms Co.; and to the following copyright owners, Ascherberg, Hopwood & Crew, Ltd., for permission to quote from *Limehouse Blues*, © 1922; Leo Feist, Inc., to quote from *No, No, Nora*, © 1923; Mills Music Company to quote from *Beale Street Mama*, © 1923 and *I Can't Give You Anything But Love*, © 1928; The Southern Music Company to quote from *Cold In Hand Blues*; The Clarence Williams Music Company to quote from *Hop Off*, © 1928; M. Witmark & Sons to quote from *You've Been a Good Ole Wagon*.

Acknowledgments are also due the editors of the *American Mercury* for permission to quote material that appeared previously in its pages.

mL
3561
.J3
S3
1975

First Paperback Printing 1975
ISBN 0-306-80001-2

This Da Capo Press edition of *Jazz: Hot and Hybrid* is an expanded version of the 1946 New and Enlarged edition, incorporating the last chapter of the 1964 edition as the penultimate chapter, and a new preface by the author.

Published by Da Capo Press, Inc.
A Subsidiary of Plenum Publishing Corporation
227 West 17th Street, New York, N.Y. 10011

To Geordie

PREFACE TO THE THIRD EDITION

When *Jazz: Hot and Hybrid* first appeared in 1938 under the imprint of Arrow Editions, a small publishing house, it was the only serious musicological study of its type in existence. There had, of course, been a great deal of previous writing about Jazz, reference to which will be found in the bibliography at the end of the book. But practically all this writing was concerned with the personalities of Jazz artists, the history of their migration from the Old South, the discography of the subject and the opinions—mostly ecstatic—of various devotees of the art. An analysis of Jazz considered as a form of music differing from other forms was badly needed. Just how much of the musical dialect of Jazz could be attributed to Black America, the area of its origin, and how much of it leaned on European traditions of musical structure? Where were the creative germs that spread to make up the musical language of Jazz? Where precisely did they come from? "Africa," would have been the commonest answer to the latter question. But this answer was faulty. Actually, Jazz was a hybrid art form, differing in many respects from the native music of Africa, and having strong roots in rural and urban America. There was a definite relationship between Jazz and certain simpler varieties of European music. There was also an obvious relationship to the popular music of the Caribbean and South America. Nevertheless, Jazz was the creation of the Black American, who used such influences as were at hand to evolve his own colorful and vital kind of music.

7

The purpose of *Jazz: Hot and Hybrid* was to demonstrate these influences and relationships and to analyse the complex musical language that had resulted.

The demonstration took the author through a study of such preceding Afro-American idioms as Ragtime, the Negro spiritual, the Latin-American tango, the archaic American cakewalk, and various more or less "pure" varieties of Jazz, including what was then known as "Hot Jazz" and the somewhat watered down variety of Jazz used by dance bands, both Black and White. There were similarities and differences to be observed in all this material, and no end of classifications and generalizations to be made.

Now, thirty-seven years later, there has been a huge proliferation of writing on the subject—most of it, as before, relating to personalities and discographies—but some small portion of it following in the musicological path laid down in *Jazz: Hot and Hybrid*. But the field of serious musicological investigation of the subject has never been overburdened with literature, and *Jazz: Hot and Hybrid* has, if I do not flatter myself unduly, remained a classic in its field. It has gone through several reprintings, each of which has constituted a new edition. The present edition is probably its last, for several reasons. Among them is that Jazz ceased to evolve around the middle 1960's because its popularity was being contested by the new arts of Rock and Country Music. Jazz, however, remains a distinct art form, and a distinct contribution of Black America to American culture.

—Winthrop Sargeant

FOREWORD TO THE 1946 EDITION

THE PRESENT VOLUME is a revision and expansion of the book that appeared in a limited edition almost ten years ago under the title *Jazz: Hot and Hybrid*. In those years the history, biography and sociology of American popular music have been considerably furthered by a number of able writers, and the documentation of recorded jazz has approached the complexity of a science. Jazz criticism, too, has filled volumes, and become one of the liveliest and most contentious fields in contemporary writing about art. The particular field that *Jazz: Hot and Hybrid* sets out to explore however, has, as far as I am aware, remained almost exclusively its own. It is not primarily a critical or a biographical or a historical book. Its purpose is descriptive. What evaluation it contains is limited mainly to the consideration of jazz as a type of art compared with other types of art. Its task has been to define jazz, to analyze its musical anatomy, to trace its origins and influences, to indicate the features that distinguish it from other kinds of music and that give it its unique place in the music of the world.

WINTHROP SARGEANT.

CONTENTS

JAZZ:
HOT AND HYBRID

Chapter 1

TERRAIN

FOR AT LEAST fifty years, American popular music has exhibited certain characteristic symptoms which have given it a distinct place in the popular music of the world. For at least twenty-five, the popular music exhibiting these symptoms has been known, more or less consistently, as jazz. In the hands of musical entertainers this music has, from time to time, undergone slight changes of style. Issuing originally from sources very foreign to the entertainment world of our big cities, the symptoms have penetrated into musical realms equally foreign. Hybrid varieties of jazz have been played, written down, danced to and otherwise participated in, by people of quite different racial and social heritages. Jazz itself has become the mainstay of several large industries.

In considering jazz broadly as the dominant language or dialect of our popular music, certain historical differences in style have always been taken for granted. Sometimes these differences have been real; sometimes they have been merely the result of changes of formula designed to create a public demand for dance bands, sheet music, phonograph records, or other products of the commercial music industry. The big divisions are fairly obvious. Our remote ancestors of the 'nineties danced the cakewalk, whose prim foursquare rhythms showed the telltale symptoms slightly but perceptibly. From the turn of the century up to the beginning of the first World War the country was swept by the curious pianistic art of ragtime. The widespread popularity of the blues during the years immediately preceding that war effected a definite change in the popular idiom, left the way open for the "sweet," song-style jazz that dominated popular music in the 'twenties. In 1935 a so-called "hot jazz" fad suddenly erupted, threatened for a time to sweep song-style jazz from popularity, brought the tastes of urban sophisticates back to a type of jazz that had flourished in the dives of New Orleans, Memphis and St. Louis even before our cake-walking ancestors first got the infection.

Some of these changes in commercial popular music have been the result of alterations in the makeup of dance and entertainment bands. Some, also, have arisen from alterations in the channels of the entertainment business itself. Ragtime, for example, reflected an era of player-pianos and barroom ditties, a period when most American towns had their own theatrical troupes, their own writers of popular music. In the theatre of the ragtime era, the rag shared honors generously with the Anglo-Celtic sentimental song and the Paris-Vienna operetta tradition. The commercial jazz of the 1920's, on the other hand, was a standardized product emanating from Broadway and the highly centralized tune-factories of Tin Pan Alley and Hollywood. It dominated the radio and movie fields to the near exclusion of all other types of popular music. One of its most characteristic features was the radio crooner whose peculiar vocal art was, in part, a technological product of the microphone.

The swing, or "hot jazz," craze which began in 1935 owed at least part of its ascendancy to the development of the phonograph. There was nothing new about hot jazz in 1935. The finest hot jazz playing had, in fact, long preceded the fad, and the phenomenon of syncopated improvisation had been going on in the deep South for at least three-quarters of a century. But people were beginning to realize that the phonograph had made available, on a mass production basis, a variety of spontaneous music that hitherto could be heard only by a fortunate, or unfortunate, few under ideal circumstances. People could now buy "swing" records where they formerly bought the rather unsatisfactory approximations of jazz which printed sheet music offered them. A new method of dissemination had made possible the sudden efflorescence of a different aspect of jazz. Where ragtime had appealed to amateur pianists, the jazz of the 1920's became highly professionalized. Hot jazz, as a nation-wide craze, was primarily the product of the phonograph and the radio.

Meanwhile the industrious research carried on by the more intellectual followers of hot jazz during the late 1930's somewhat changed the accepted picture of American popular music. Obscure aficionados of the more primitive types of pure Negroid improvisation became more vocal. Critics like Wilder Hobson, Paul Eduard Miller, Charles Edward Smith, Frederic Ramsey and the European pundits Hugues Panassié and Robert Goffin battled manfully for the cause of spontaneous, improvised jazz as opposed to the slick, commonplace jazz of the big popular entertainment industry. They pointed out that a type of jazz existed in comparative obscurity that was being played not so much for commercial exploitation, as for the enjoyment of the players themselves and of a few of their sincere followers. This type of jazz was free of the over-polished tricks and dreary formulas of the commercial product, and it had a certain artistic integrity. It was heard, not in fashionable ballrooms and ornate movie palaces, but in private get-togethers, college house parties, humble Negro slums and—occasionally—on obscure phonograph records. Its freshness and exuberance, which gave it something of the naïve charm of primitive painting, proved it to be the vital source from which more successful commercial bands were drawing all of their more imaginative tricks and idioms.

In seeking for the roots of this improvised type of jazz, the researchers of the late 1930's unearthed a tradition that had long been obscured by the ballyhoo of the commercial dance-band industry. This tradition had run parallel to the history of commercial popular music and had kept its vigor and characteristic quality more or less consistently since the turn of the century. The tradition was largely a Negro affair, and had its origins apparently in the illiterate improvisations of the New Orleans Negroes around 1900. Much that has been written about this tradition is overenthusiastic, and some of it misleading. The characteristic features of the jazz musical dialect were not invented overnight by the colorful and now legendary New Orleans trumpeter Buddy Bolden who seems to be regarded by hot jazz aesthetes as the Giovanni da Palestrina of jazz. They had probably existed in various forms for at least a generation before Bolden's time. But the type of improvised instrumental jazz that was handed down by Bolden to such celebrated New Orleans Negro musicians as Joseph "King" Oliver, Willie "Bunk" Johnson and Louis "Satchel Mouth" Armstrong undoubtedly constituted a special American art form. If it was not the only type of jazz America produced during the first decades of the century, it was by all odds the best, the purest and the most artistically consistent. New Orleans had produced an integrated tradition of jazz performance, which was something the trick commercial bands with their changing fads and fashions, had never attained. In 1914 a white product of this Negro tradition, the famous Original Dixieland Jazz Band, moved north and gave Chicagoans and New Yorkers a foretaste of the New Orleans style. A year later the tradition, carried by other itinerant artists like Armstrong, Oliver, and the saxophonist Sydney Bechet, moved up the Mississippi and settled in Chicago where it produced between 1918 and 1928 what has since become known as the Chicago style. Native Chicago musicians, many of them whites like Dave Tough, Jack Teagarden and the famous "Bix" Beiderbecke, became part of the tradition, which by 1930 moved on to New York and began to dissipate itself somewhat by contact with the big commercial entertainment world. By 1935, just as the famous Chicago clarinetist Benny Goodman was reaching the peak of his popularity, America suddenly became aware of the New Orleans-Chicago style, which was now dubbed "swing" in contradistinction to the "sweet" music most people thought of as jazz. During the "swing" fad, New Orleans-Chicago jazz became immensely popular, highly successful and shamelessly imitated and exploited. In the process it became commercialized and lost most of the naïve, spontaneous character for which connoisseurs had originally admired it. One by-product of this situation was a nostalgic attempt on the part of disappointed hot jazz enthusiasts to recapture the original New Orleans style. None of the original New Orleans bands had ever made phonograph records. But many of the men who played in them were still alive. Tracing them down with great pains, the hot enthusiasts banded them together and made, through various channels, a considerable number of recordings. Future music historians will owe them a great deal of gratitude. For these records, many of them privately made by old-time artists like "Bunk" Johnson and "Jelly Roll" Morton, at least offer us some clues as to how the jazz of New Orleans in 1910 actually sounded.

It is customary, in popular writing, to place the origin of the jazz idiom in New Orleans sometime in the late 1890's. But, as we shall see later on, an examination of the structure of Southern Negro secular and religious music shows that most of the essential elements of jazz are far older than the present century. Even in the limited chronicles offered by printed commercial sheet music, we find the traces of these elements persistently recorded as early as 1900 in the rags and songs of composers like Scott Joplin and Rosamund Johnson. They may well have been present in the music of the earliest minstrel shows, and of the plantation darky shows after which they were patterned.

The printed versions of the old minstrel songs offer, of course, a very dubious key to what was actually sung in the heat of performance. If the 1840's had had the benefit of the phonograph, we might have a very different and much more accurate idea of what early Afro-American entertainment and dance music sounded like. As it is, we must depend principally on conjecture and on second-hand reports. Those who can remember minstrelsy prior to 1900 seem agreed that minstrel music was characterized by something of the spontaneity and rhythmic vitality that has always been associated with the music of the Negro. Moreover, enough evidence has leaked down even in the comparatively rigid channels of printed music to lend support to the idea that the minstrels employed an idiom related to jazz. Such early "coon songs" as *Turkey in the Straw* which, according to records, made its first appearance under the title *Old Zip Coon* in 1834, contain marks in accent and phraseology of the idiom that was later to dominate our popular music.

While jazz as a distinct type of music is probably older than the jazz band or the period sometimes referred to as the "jazz age," it is also true that the jazz idiom finds expression over a somewhat larger territory than that traversed by the music of the modern jazz orchestra. A thorough consideration of the subject cannot limit itself to this single facet of the phenomenon without the danger of arriving at very superficial conclusions. The commercial jazz band of our music halls, night clubs and hot spots, is the most obvious but not necessarily the most basic manifestation of the idiom. And even here there are distinctions. "Hot jazz" differs radically from the "sweet" jazz of the polite dance ensemble. Moreover, jazz, even in this limited field, is not entirely a matter of music. Jazz begets dancing, and the dancing associated with it exhibits certain aesthetic and rhythmic similarities to the performances of its musicians. In its simplest form this dancing may amount merely to unconscious nodding and foot-jiggling on the part of someone listening to a jazz performance. It passes to a somewhat more picturesque stage in the vacant-minded, hypnotized "shagging" of the adolescent "jitterbug" whose pseudo-primitive orgies were such a prominent feature of the "swing" fad. A somewhat more severe and systematized variety of the same phenomenon may be found in the more or less spontaneous walking-patterns of the average polite dance floor. In a Negro dance hall with a hot orchestra the dance patterns are apt to involve not only feet but arms, hips and practically every other moveable part of the human anatomy

JAZZ: HOT AND HYBRID

Then there is the specialized art of tap-dancing, which among Americans has been developed into a branch of jazz, its rhythms falling into patterns similar to, and often even more complex and delicate than, those of the jazz drummer.

Outside the ballroom and the field of commercial entertainment the jazz idiom flowers in a dozen other forms. It can be traced not only to the secular celebrations of the Southern Negroes, but to their religious ceremonies. Its ingredients are found not only in Negro music, but, as we shall see, in the inflections of Negro speech. Influences from Africa have been much talked about. A very few of these influences can be given documentary proof. At one end of the gamut of jazz phenomena highbrow composers will be found trying to build symphonies, concertos and rhapsodies with jazz ingredients. At the other end lie the whooping and drumming of primitive African tribes. Between these two extremes there has grown a main stem of Afro-American musical expression, of which the Southern "spiritual" is one outgrowth, the Creole music of Haiti, Cuba and Brazil another, the sophisticated jazz of our big cities merely an important branch. Thus, depending on how you look at it, jazz is either a large phenomenon penetrating a dozen different arts and fields of human activity, or (by a more restricted definition) a type of popular band music related to a larger and more inclusive manifestation.

Much has been written about the aesthetic aspects of jazz. Its peculiarities as an art form, its deviations from the conventions of European concert and folk music, its social and cultural implications, its origins and its future possibilities have been widely discussed by critics, musicians, journalists and dilettantes. Its essential nature has always proved somewhat elusive and difficult to define. It has never seemed to fit precisely the more familiar aesthetics of the musical art as Europeans and American "highbrows" have known it. It has been called a folk music. Yet it is in several important respects unlike any of the folk music of the Western peoples. It has been hailed as the music of the future—as in some way a potential successor to the great European musical tradition of the past two or three centuries. Yet its resemblances to the music of this tradition are superficial. It is not, properly speaking, a type of concert music at all. Most of its vitality and charm is lost if it is played deliberately before large audiences as symphonies and operas are played. And it is completely lacking in the intellectual and structural features that sustain the interest of a cultivated "highbrow" musical audience over long periods of time.

Its melodies are not handed down comparatively intact from generation to generation as are most folk melodies. Nor do the people who create it, or who participate in its creation, fall neatly into the categories—composer, performer, audience— that are associated with the production of concert or operatic music. In jazz the categories are indistinct. A tune may be "composed," as we understand the term, by a Tin Pan Alley songwriter. In itself it will, in most cases, be a trivial, catchy bit of melody written according to a rather unimaginative formula, and destined to be forgotten within a few months of its appearance. This rather commonplace melody may then reach the hands of a clever arranger with a fund of practical musicianship and a good ear for instrumental effect. The arranger will dress it up with adroit modulations and slick instrumentation, giving it a semblance of extended form and forestalling its inherent monotony with various recipes for con- trast. Next, the composition, as it may now be termed, passes into the hands of one of the more pretentious dance orchestras and is carefully rehearsed. The players, however, do not stick to the letter of the arranger's score as symphonic musicians do to the notes of a symphony or a concerto. They worry and cajole the rhythms and phrases of their solos, extemporizing here and there, introducing solo "breaks," and otherwise ornamenting the printed skeleton that has been provided for their collective guidance.

Or to consider another possibility: The songwriter's tune, or some other tune—the source does not matter provided it is in duple or quadruple meter—is heard by the musically illiterate trumpeter of a small "hot" ensemble. This musician—much freer than his colleagues in the "sweet" band above—makes the snatch of melody a sort of text for a musical sermon. Without the benefits or disadvantages of deliberate rehearsal, he varies the pattern of the melody, tortures it this way and that, leaves it for melodic inspirations of his own, returns to it again, tosses it back and forth among his colleagues who tear it up into all sorts of unrecognizable melodic shapes.

In both these cases the interesting ingredients of the music are provided by the performers, and (perhaps less often) by the arrangers. The composer, that towering artistic figure of concert music, occupies here a very lowly if not entirely unnecessary role. In the end his "composition" is almost completely lost sight of, or at best serves as a mere framework on which more interesting things are hung.

Nor is the audience a passive and purely receptive element in this creative process. If it dances, which in many cases it does, it is occupied no less than the musicians in building extemporaneous rhythmic patterns, patterns of movement, and even sometimes of percussive sound. Its contribution is an organic part of the phenomenon, following with somewhat different means, the same essential system of rhythmic forms as that employed by the player. Here we are, of course, still considering jazz in its restricted definition—as a variety of dance music. But the same peculiarities of extemporaneous creation and of audience participation, the same type of rhythmic and melodic pattern-building, will be found in all the more primitive social celebrations of the American Negro. A Negro "shoutin'" congregation in church, for example, will follow the same general procedure, building its service extemporaneously into a rhythmo-dramatic work of art with many component designs indistinguishable from those of the dance hall. We are faced here with an entirely new wrinkle in musical aesthetics.

There has been a great deal of dubious and highly confusing writing around the subject of jazz. Probably no musical movement in history has been made the object of more leaky speculation. Just after the first World War it was fashionable for a time to maintain that jazz, with its mechanically throbbing fundamental rhythm, somehow represented or expressed the machine age in music. It was also fashionable to maintain that jazz, owing to the rhythmic freedom and abandon of its upper melodic voices, represented the bacchanalian moral laxity of the post-war world. Because jazz reached its first tremendous wave of popularity during the first World War, many people maintained that jazz was somehow expressing an emotional escape from the tension of the battlefield. It was not long afterward that Marxist ideologists were discovering that jazz was really the music of the downtrodden proletariat, and that the abandon, regularity (or something) of its rhythm was really a satirical, martial (or something) protest against the evils of capitalist society. Many people, of course, maintained that jazz was an immoral influence on the youth of the land. Many detected in its carefree melodies a symbolic language of satire in which the embittered Negro was expressing his dislike for his white neighbors. Some even regarded the whole thing as a Jewish plot.

It is undoubtedly true that social conditions and prevailing attitudes of mind have now and then created a specially strong popular demand for jazz, just as they might have created a popular interest in surrealism or billiards. Jazz may do certain things to certain people. People in certain states of mind may be attracted by jazz. But the attempt to link up jazz to moral and social ideas, or to the *Weltanschauung* of modern civilization has proved on the whole a rather barren intellectual pastime, and has tended to disappear from most recent writing on the subject. It has never contributed an iota of clarification to the musical and aesthetic question "What is jazz?"

Even in the technical and aesthetic fields discussion has too often tended to obscure rather than clarify fundamentals. At one time it was customary to think of the Tin Pan Alley tunesmith as the glorious fountainhead of our popular music. Later it became fashionable to consider jazz as purely a matter of improvisation (which very little of it actually is), and to refer in lofty whispers to the "creative genius" of every simple-minded honky-tonk trumpeter. The admirers of *"le jazz hot"* have a habit of writing about jazz in a language which, for sheer obscurity, pomposity and purpleness, frequently surpasses that of our most impenetrable highbrow music criticism. But whatever the faults of the jazz-as-a-fine-art cult may be, it has created a literature about jazz which considers jazz as a self-contained type of music with its own standards and its own aesthetic. Nowadays nobody any longer believes, for example, that jazz is merely a satirical distortion of European-style music. The silly practice of "jazzing the classics," in which jazz appears as a sort of musical caricature, once lent weight to the idea that the syncopations of jazz were primarily intended as humor. "Jazzing the classics" will always strike the cultivated listener as musical bad taste, not because of what it does to the classics (which survive it well enough) but because of what it does to the jazz. To extract a small tune from the intricate framework of a symphony and subject it to jazz variations is no crime. But to pretend that you are thereby "jazzing" (or in some way manipulating) the symphony itself, is to be guilty of misrepresentation of an extremely callow sort. Though their tunes may be, symphonies, sonatas and fugues are simply not jazzable.

Any serious consideration of the whole subject of jazz must rest on precise definitions which writers on the subject have too often disregarded. What is jazz? When three or four Negro musicians get together in a New Orleans dive and loose their enthusiasms in a collective improvisation, does that constitute jazz? And if so, when a commercial Tin Pan Alley tunesmith writes a melody down on paper and (if he is a sufficiently good musician) an accompaniment, is that jazz? Is jazz, as Paul Whiteman once wrote, "not the thing said, but the manner of saying it?" Or is it, as Gershwin and others have attempted to make it, a valuable ingredient of "highbrow" compositions like rhapsodies and operas? Is the ragtime of the period preceding the first World War a type of jazz? Is jazz the system of rhythmic and harmonic formulas exhibited in the average piece of popular sheet music, or the carefully rehearsed and arranged body of sound that issues from a fashionable dance orchestra, or, as the "hot jazz" enthusiasts will have it, the extemporaneous product of an improvising ensemble? Are all these merely different varieties of jazz? Or is jazz some sort of essential element that manifests itself in one way or another in all these varied forms or results of musical activity?

Underlying much of this confusion is the disregard of a distinction which must be clearly made in any discussion relating to the aesthetics of non-European music and of folk music in general, the distinction between music itself and the usually somewhat inaccurate representation of music that is achieved in symbols written or printed on paper. Music itself has existence only when it sounds. Its materials are time-values and vibration frequencies produced by setting various resonant substances—catgut, columns of air, pieces of metal, vocal cords —in motion. To preserve it for succeeding generations, and to fix relationships so that complex musical forms may be planned in detail before they are actually made concrete in sound (we call the process musical composition), various expedients have been employed. One of the most important and complex of these expedients is modern musical notation. Even in discussing the European concert art, in connection with which this system of notation was specially devised, it is sometimes dangerous to confuse the printed symbol with the ephemeral and elusive sound-value which it very roughly represents. In considering folk music, or other music not constructed with reference to such a standardized system, the confusion is likely to result in a complete misconception of the nature of the music itself.

Chapter 2

THE AESTHETICS OF FOLK MUSIC

ANYONE who has attempted to transcribe folk music, or the music of Oriental nations, in terms of our musical notation has observed that the symbols traditionally used by us in writing music are very imperfectly suited to such purposes. The problem is somewhat similar to that of recording in printed words the precise sound values of a dialect only remotely related to the language for which the system of writing was created. The task of the musical transcriber is, indeed, more difficult than the comparison would indicate, since music involves a far more complex group of important distinctions in the realm of sound than language does.

The transcriber of even such familiar musical idioms as are represented in Spanish or Hungarian folk songs finds himself confronted with a myriad of small peculiarities—slight deviations from conventional intonation, *portamentos*, or "scoops," *rubatos*, or irregularities of tempo and rhythm, subtleties of accentuation and tone-coloring—that defy precise expression in our notational system. Even among the various types of European concert music (especially in those more directly influenced by folk idioms), there are apt to be found certain stylistic ingredients that submit only awkwardly to printed representation. Among the more familiar of these are the cadential *fermatas* of the conventional Italian operatic aria, the advanced second beat of the properly performed Viennese waltz, the *rubatos* traditional in the performance of Chopin's piano pieces and the violent changes of tempo peculiar to music of Hungarian flavor as represented in popular works by Brahms and Liszt. In each case these are integral and essential elements of the music as performed. Yet the written page offers only a vague approximation of their actual nature. In music less related to the European concert art the discrepancies between musical actuality and the black-and-white diagrams of musical scoring are very much more in evidence.

Our musical notation describes the sound-values of music in relation to such co-ordinates as duration, pitch and intensity. On the printed page a sound is plotted much as a mathematician would plot a point or a tendency upon a graph. From a mathematical point of view, however, notation is exceedingly crude and inexact. By exact interpretation of the notational symbols, for example, a given note will remain at a constant pitch and at a constant degree of loudness and softness throughout its duration. Actually this is seldom the case. If a violinist plays it or a singer sings it, its loudness may alter considerably during its passage. Its middle may be louder or softer than its beginning or its end. But this change in loudness is seldom indicated in print. If the performer gives the note the emotional color imparted by *vibrato,* its pitch may oscillate considerably during its passage. Notation does not possess any method of indicating the degree or rapidity of this oscillation. When one considers the factors that enter with the transition from one note to another, one finds the notational scheme at even more striking variance with musical actuality. The transition is, in fact, not indicated at all. Its starting point and its ultimate goal are symbolized by two successive notes. But a violinist will make continuous use of little slides between notes—not sufficiently obvious to constitute real *portamentos* but nevertheless quite noticeable. They form a very important factor in the traditional interpretation of all violin passages, and the excellence of a violinist's musicianship is often gauged by the taste he exhibits in the use of them. Singers, too, by necessity, "scoop" more or less audibly to and from every note of a legato passage. These things are part of the tradition of music as sound. They are not conveyed to the interpreter by notation but by his experience of the living language of music.

Essentially then notation is a convention by which the general proportions of a composition may be roughly described. It is not to be confused with music itself. It is merely the blue-print from which music may be constructed. It has its advantages as an expedient for the preservation of the structural ideas of composers and as an aid in the manipulation of musical proportions; but music itself remains a transient experience of ephemeral designs in values of time, a process of change in which each element passes from the future into the past, dying at the instant of its birth, tangible only as a momentary oscillation of air particles.

If I seem to digress here into the general field of musical aesthetics, it is only because these discrepancies are so often ignored by writers on music as to constitute a continual source of muddlement. The distinction here indicated is not only valuable to our discussion in that it points to the untrustworthiness and inaccuracy of notation as a conveyance for jazz; it is also important as indicating a difference of attitude toward the art of music between us, whose ideas of music are often colored by notational considerations, and the musically illiterate folk artist whose ideas of music are not so colored.

There can be no doubt that, while the notational system as an implement has contributed greatly to the complexity and nobility of Western musical expression, it has also exercised certain limiting influences upon that expression. Our composers, while able by its means to create and adjust the ingredients of such monumental forms as the symphony and the music-drama, have at the same time been constrained to write the type of music that may be most readily expressed in terms of notation. The improvisatory freedom of the folk-musician is foreign to the art of concert music. We have made a distinction, unknown alike to the primitive folk musician and to the musician of non-European musical cultures, between the composer—the creator of elaborate plans for musical performance—and the interpretative artist whose function it is to embody the conceptions of the composer in sound. The noblest department of Western concert music has become the art of composition. This art of composition is not concerned directly with the creation of music (*i.e.* sound) but rather with the creation of plans from which music may be subsequently created. In its domination by the *planner* rather than the *manipulator* our musical system is unique; and its peculiarities have obscured, for many of us, the fundamental nature of musical expression. In its primitive essentials the art of music has nothing whatever to do with the institution of the composer. Actually improvisation—the art of creating music directly with vocal or instrumental means—is far more fundamental to music than is the complex, difficult and specialized art of planning compositions on paper.

THE AESTHETICS OF FOLK MUSIC

We do not stop to think, when we consider the creative activity of a Beethoven or a Bach that these artists were using an already highly developed musical language that, as a whole, can be traced to improvisatory beginnings. I do not refer here to the occasional use of contemporary folk idioms that are to be found in the work of almost every composer, but to the very substance in which the composer embodies his musical thought. Beethoven was the heir to a traditional language of sound that had been previously developed by Haydn, Mozart, Bach, and others, who were in turn indebted for their means of expression to the Italian contrapuntal style of a century before, to the Lutheran chorale, to the Gregorian chant, to the folk music of mediaeval Europe and to other sources. Of these the Italian contrapuntal style was itself evolved from various sources to which instrumental and choral improvisation contributed. The Lutheran chorale had its roots equally in the improvisatory singing of masses of people, and the Gregorian chant is the lineal descendant of music that was created at a time before notation and the composer were ever heard of. If we may alter the familiar opening of Genesis to suit yet another connotation: "In the beginning was improvisation." The composer came later as the flower of an altogether special type of musical art in which the creative functions had become split into the departments of "composition" and "interpretation."

Habituated to thinking in terms of composers and performers, the Western music-lover does not readily picture to himself an art of music without composers, an art of which the individual works are not treasured up and perpetuated for posterity's benefit, an art in which creation and performance are one and occur at the same instant. Yet the great bulk of the human race creates and enjoys its music precisely after this fashion. And the roots even of Western music lie deeply imbedded in the same improvisatory process. Habitually the Western music-lover thinks of improvisation as a rambling musical pastime for the executive artist, or as a peculiarity of "primitive" (meaning childishly simple) music. Yet even a cursory study of the music of such Oriental cultures as those of India or Arabia, reveals that the art of improvisation may achieve certain complexities unknown to our own music, that whole musical cultures have existed, enlisting the services of renowned executants—even of critics and prolific writers on musicology and musical aesthetics—and yet have been wholly without that particular activity which we designate as musical composition.

What, then, is the essential nature of music? What are the elements common to all types of musical expression from the Neapolitan folk song and the primitive piping and drumming of the South Sea Islander to the highly developed improvisations of the Orient and the great composer-dominated art of modern Europe? A conclusive and detailed answer to that would be a large order—a larger one than we need attempt for our present purposes. A few basic considerations stand out fairly obviously, however. First, that music in all its essential aspects is concerned with the manipulation of sound. Second, that it is a social activity demanding the participation of masses of human beings, whether as witnesses to or creators of its immediate performance, or as anonymous contributors to the language it takes shape in. Certain of its manifestations may demand the special ministrations of composers, of improvisatory virtuosos, the assistance of printed records, of theoretical systems, and of specialists whose functions are concerned with the elaboration and conservation of these. But above all such peculiarities stands the consideration of music as a socially evolved phenomenon, something similar in a different medium to what Walt Whitman had in mind when he wrote, "Literature is great; language is greater."

The bearing of all this on any discussion of folk music is obvious. Folk music is the anonymous and musically illiterate expression of a whole people. Of all types of music it is the most directly social in origin. It is usually closely bound up with such social functions as lovemaking, dancing, communal labor, and religious worship. No primitive or agrarian society is without it. It is evolved for the communicative needs of mankind as surely and inevitably as language is evolved, and like language, with which it is often closely related in matters of cadence and inflection, it falls into distinct idioms and dialects peculiar to given regions and racial heritages. Being the expression of the musically illiterate it is, of course, largely improvisatory in character.

The folk music of the American Negro, with which we are here concerned, is perhaps more directly improvisatory than any of the European folk musics. Spirituals and secular songs have been collected and published from time to time, and have even entered the repertoire of the sophisticated concert singer. This, to the superficial observer, has given them the status of "compositions," that is, of fixed musical creations designed to be "interpreted" according to the conventions of our concert art. This notion, as has often been pointed out by those familiar at first hand with Negro musical expression, is an essential misunderstanding of their nature and function. While certain spirituals and secular tunes are passed about and handed down relatively intact, they are seldom sung twice in exactly the same manner by the naïve, rural Negroes who create them. They are varied and re-created incessantly. Every meeting of a "shoutin' " congregation will evolve a few new spirituals, a few variants of old ones and a welter of embryonic material, half speech, half song, that is of great musical interest and perfectly suited to its extemporaneous purpose, but wholly without the stability we associate with the term "composition as we apply it to, say, a hymn tune.

The rural Negro congregation does not sing hymns; it creates the musical elements of a whole religious ceremony on the spur of the moment. It may commence with a prayer or a sermon in which the preacher gradually, under the stress of religious fervor, merges his spoken monologue with a type of declamation already recognizable, in its insistent rhythms and scalar peculiarities, as music of a sort. To his solo the congregation will contribute an accompaniment of antiphonal "ain't it so's!" and "hallelujah's!" of punctuating grunts, hand clappings and foot stampings. Gradually, in this process, distinct and recognizable musical creations will take shape, some of them perhaps familiar in spots, some of them entirely new —"spirituals" if you wish to call them that, but very different musical experiences from the polite, arranged, and rehearsed songs with piano accompaniment that go by that title in the concert hall.

The late Natalie Curtis-Burlin, an acute observer of the musical habits of the deep South, has described this phenomenon as well as anyone in her *Hampton Collection of Negro Folk Songs*. "Often in the South," she writes, "I heard this same strange breathless effect of a song being born among a group simultaneously, descending, as it were, from the air.

36

THE AESTHETICS OF FOLK MUSIC

On a suffocatingly hot July Sunday in Virginia, in a little ramshackle meeting-house that we had approached over a blinding road nearly a foot deep in dust, a number of rural Negroes had gathered from an outlying farm, dressed all in their dust-stained Sunday best for the never-to-be-omitted Sabbath service. Their intense and genuine piety with its almost barbaric wealth of emotion could not but touch a visitor from the cold North. The poverty of the little church was in itself a mute appeal for sympathy. A gaudy and some-what ragged red tablecloth covered the crude pulpit on which rested a huge and very battered Bible—it had probably sustained many vigorous thumps during the high-flown exhortations of the gilt-spectacled preacher. A crazy lamp, tilted sideways, hung from the middle of the ceiling. Through the broken window-shutters (powerless to keep out the diamond glare of the morning sun) came slits of light that slanted in syncopated angles over the swarthy people, motes dancing in the beams. No breeze; the sticky heat was motionless; from afar came a faint sound of chickens clucking in the dust. Service had already begun before we came, and the congregation, silent and devout, sat in rows on rough backless benches. The preacher now exhorted his flock to prayer and the people with one movement surged forward from the benches and down onto their knees, every black head deep-bowed in an abandonment of devotion. Then the preacher began in a quavering voice a long supplication. Here and there came an uncontrollable cough from some kneeling penitent or the sudden squall of a restless child; and now and again an ejaculation, warm with entreaty, 'O Lord!' or a muttered 'Amen, Amen'—all against the background of the praying, endless praying.

"Minutes passed, long minutes of strange intensity. The mutterings, the ejaculations, grew louder, more dramatic, till suddenly I felt the creative thrill dart through the people like an electric vibration, that same half-audible hum arose—emotion was gathering atmospherically as clouds gather—and then, up from the depths of some 'sinner's' remorse and imploring came a pitiful little plea, a real Negro 'moan,' sobbed in musical cadence. From somewhere in that bowed gathering another voice improvised a response; the plea sounded again, louder this time and more impassioned; then other voices joined in the answer, shaping it into a musical phrase; and so, before our ears, as one might say, from this molten metal of music a new song was smithied out, composed then and there by no one in particular and by everyone in general."

Here we have what some would describe as the evolution of a spiritual. The word "evolution," however, implies that the events described were merely a formative process from which emerged a completed product—a spiritual, a "composition" in the Western sense, something that could be written down, or at least remembered and made the subject of future "interpretations." It is extremely doubtful, however, that the primitive Negro congregation considered it in any such light. The improvised work of art so created suited its own time and place and the emotions of its creators at the time of its evolvement. It was important as a part of that particular service. Other services would build up different efflorescences of tone and rhythm. The process was not one of striving toward a creative goal, but was in itself a fully finished work of art, a perfect example of the Negro's improvisatory type of expression. A musical ethnographer, present at the time, might have written down some phrases of the ultimate crystallization and called them a spiritual. But such notational recording would do little justice to the atmosphere of breathless expectancy, to the surge of spontaneous emotional expression that the scene itself contained for those who participated in it.

*   *   *   *   *

This different, and perhaps more fundamental, relation in which the Negro stands to his own musical art is by no means limited to the field of religious worship. His art is not something to be looked at or listened to, but something to be participated in, something to be done. Except where the white man intrudes his objective attitude and looks at it from the outside, it has no audience—unless one considers the creators themselves in that capacity. And this is as true in the dance halls of Harlem and Chicago's South Side as it is in the rural Negro churches of central Alabama. Anyone who has visited a ballroom frequented exclusively by Negroes cannot but have been impressed by the close and spontaneous rapport between the dancers on the floor and the musicians in the orchestra. The element of improvisation is not limited to the playing of the musicians, nor is their function in relation to the whole proceeding any different from that of the dancers except in the fact that they happen to be blowing or thumping instruments where the dancers are using their bodies and voices and thumping the floor with their feet. The essence of all this activity, as in the church, is the element of participation. Again a work of art is being built at the moment for the emotional needs of the moment, contributed to by everyone present. The Negro's musical art may be experienced in sacred or profane surroundings. From the purely aesthetic point of view its manifestations in both are strikingly similar.

39

JAZZ: HOT AND HYBRID

To a certain extent these Negroid artistic conventions are also typical of the sophisticated jazz of our big cities. Tin Pan Alley and the fashionable night club have taken over not only the Negro's musical idioms, but something of the social behavior that goes with them. Here, of course, we have a type of music more involved in its creative process than that of the shoutin' congregation or the small back-alley dance dive. This dance music of America's large cities is composed by well-known people with imposing studio-suites in Hollywood or on Broadway. It is published in sheet music form by large business concerns, and its melodies are "interpreted" by large dance orchestras in varying degrees of "arrangement." The "hot" ensemble whose ubiquitous musical hysteria first became popular under the name "swing," makes, of course, little compromise with Western musical convention. Its product is, or is supposed to be, purely improvisatory. But even to the more deliberate type of "sweet" jazz, some measure of the Negroid aesthetic still applies. Even the smart roof garden of a New York hotel, with the languid and redundant strains of a polite dance orchestra and a slow-moving crowd of hypnotized collegians, offers a spectacle of sexual ceremony not essentially different from the Negro's. The satin-gowned debutante adjusts her movements to those of her partner by a species of improvisation, while he glides along as the impulse of the moment and the spatial limitations of the dance floor dictate. The musicians who accompany them improvise to a certain extent—as much, at any rate, as the complexities of rehearsed and large-scale jazz will permit. And nothing could be duller than the function of an "audience" at this spectacle if there should, by any chance, be such a passive and purely receptive element present. Even here the routine skeleton of Tin Pan Alley sheet-music has been forgotten in the wealth of improvisatory material that has been imposed upon it. Its composer's contribution represents only a feeble portion of the ultimate performance. Again, despite certain superficial differences, we have the phenomenon of mass improvisation.

*   *   *   *   *

In this particular sort of musical creation, musical notation —with its attendant phenomenon, the composer—plays, as we have seen, very little part. The printed page—all-important adjunct to the "permanence" of Western music—is not essential to jazz even in its more refined manifestations. And, as might be expected, even the most deliberate and systematic "sweet" jazz presents a continuous array of melodic, harmonic and rhythmic features that cannot even be hinted at in notational terms.

It is for this reason that printed versions of spirituals and jazz offer a very dubious foundation for a study of Negroid, or Negro-influenced music. Printed collections of spirituals are numerous. But even at the hands of capable transcribers, like Natalie Curtis-Burlin, Nathaniel Dett, and Nicholas J. G. Ballanta-Taylor, much of the rhythmic and melodic detail of the original is inevitably lost. The notated spiritual only approximates the original version, leaving large gaps to be filled in by the memory or imagination of the reader. Too often, lacking the memory of actual Negro performance, the reader uses his imagination, and, because that accords with his musical experience, fills in the gaps with European equivalents. The result is far removed from the original music. While even the highly conscientious transcriber is faced here with insuper-

able difficulties, there can be little doubt that the great mass
of spiritual transcription which has been going on steadily since
the Civil War, has been far from accurate, even within the
limited possibilities of accuracy that the notational system
offers. Characteristic Negro elements have undoubtedly been
suppressed as "vulgar." It has been assumed that what does
not accord with the white man's musical conceptions is merely
the fruit of inexpertness: that the Negro tries to achieve
a perfect composition somewhat resembling a commonplace hymn-tune, and because of his propensity to rhythmic
and intonational aberration, cannot quite succeed in doing it. Spiritual collections are filled with prettified and
"improved" compositions that are the fruit of this attitude,
and they not infrequently resemble commonplace hymn-
tunes.

There has been a great deal of controversy recently over the
question of the white or Negro "origin" of the spirituals. The
problem of white vs. Negro influence in the Negroid music
of the South is an interesting one. Unfortunately most of the
discussion to date on this subject (see George Pullen Jackson:
White Spirituals in the Southern Uplands, etc.) has tended to
revolve, not around the Negroid music itself, but around the
extremely untrustworthy examples of Negro spirituals fur-
nished in the published collections. It may be—in fact it
would seem almost inevitable—that here and there a White
hymn tune has crept into the texture of a Negro religious
improvisation, been remembered, repeated, heard by some
folklorist and transcribed back into the notation of the White
man's vocabulary. White influence is undoubtedly to be discerned in the spirituals. But the crux of the problem—if White
origin there be—lies in demonstrating similarities or differences

between the actual *music* (*i.e.*, performance) of the American Negro, and that of his white neighbors.

Undoubtedly a somewhat similar state of affairs has obtained in the field of published jazz, though here the supposed "vulgarity" of Negro rhythmic abandon has not stood so much in the way of accuracy. Negro improvisation has been a wholesale source of published Tin Pan Alley song and dance music at least since the early 'nineties. Establishments like Babe Connor's celebrated Negro brothel in St. Louis were frequented by the minstrel song pirates of the 'eighties, and many a song hit of the period originated in the back streets of New Orleans and Memphis. The song rage of 1891, *Ta-ra-ra-boom-de-ay,* doesn't sound much like jazz today, but it is supposed to have originated in Babe Connor's place. The ragtime piano playing that the white pianist Ben Harney introduced to New York in 1897 probably sounded a good deal like the early jazz pianism that the Negro "Jelly Roll" Morton was thumping out in New Orleans houses of prostitution. To New Yorkers it sounded novel enough to create a sensation, and the literate musicians of Tin Pan Alley were soon getting some of its features down on paper. Harney subsequently even wrote a treatise on ragtime in which some of the more elementary rhythmic aberrations of Negro pianism were rather tentatively recorded. Borrowing little by little from the Negro style, the rag composers of the early 1900s created a tradition of piano composition which lasted at least until the time of Zez Confrey's famous *Kitten on the Keys* (1922), and which, rhythmically, was the most intricate art ever set down on paper by popular composers in this country.

The question will arise in thoughtful minds whether the Negroid jazz idiom was not fairly constant in its technical features even from the time of Babe Connors. It is quite possible that the pale and tentative character of ragtime's early rhythmic excursions was to a certain extent the result of inaccurate transcription, conveying only a small part of the original Negro style after which these excursions were patterned. This point is a legitimate subject for debate since the music in question was evolved before the phonograph came into general use. But, as we shall see later on, notated examples of "secondary rag"—that supposed peculiarity of "jazz" as distinguished from "ragtime"—are to be found here and there in printed popular music far antedating the present century. There is, at any rate, no possibility of doubting that Negro music, then as today, defied transcription of many of its characteristic features.

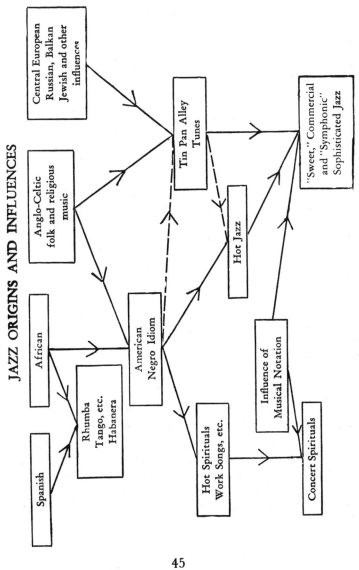

JAZZ ORIGINS AND INFLUENCES

Chapter 3

CLASSIFICATIONS AND DEFINITIONS

THE AMERICAN NEGRO'S music has usually been classified according to the social function in connection with which it has appeared. The music of the dance-hall has been known as "jazz" or "ragtime"; that of the religious service as "spirituals"; that accompanying the labor of the cotton fields and the chain-gangs as "work songs." "Blues" has been the term applied to a certain variety of secular song of lamentation. This classification is perhaps not without its usefulness in certain connections, but from the purely musical point of view it is somewhat unsatisfactory. Not only does the musical expression included under these categories overlap from one to the other, obscuring any precise lines of demarcation, but the categories themselves encompass types of music that are essentially different from each other. Thus a "spiritual" may be (1) the spontaneous expression of a shoutin' congregation in the act of worship; (2) a more or less traditional melody that is made the subject of repeated and differing versions by such a congregation; (3) a melody of similar type that has been taken over by a more or less musically sophisticated Negro chorus, carefully rehearsed and performed in the concert hall; (4) a religious song, originally of improvised character, that has been written down, given "form" and a piano accompaniment by a musically educated person and presented on the program of

46

some well-known Negro baritone or tenor; (5) a religious composition written by a white or other sophisticated musician in imitation of the Negro idiom; (6) a white hymn tune that has got woven into the fabric of a Negro religious service, been remembered by someone and transcribed back into the notation of the white man's vocabulary; and, no doubt, several other things. "Jazz" may include: (1) the sort of spontaneous improvisation known as "hot" jazz; (2) the rehearsed music played by a large professional dance orchestra in pseudo-Negroid manner including occasional solos and "breaks" that are technically "hot"; (3) rehearsed music by a sophisticated orchestra based on Tin Pan Alley tunes of purely European character which are subjected to the process known as "jazz-ing"; (4) the same type of music based on a tune pirated from the work of some classical composer; (5) something written down on paper by a Tin Pan Alley composer in imitation of the Negro method of playing, and so on.

The only outstanding musical difference between these two categories is that the spirituals are preponderantly vocal and that jazz is preponderantly instrumental, and this far from absolute distinction is of slight importance in its bearing on musical form and style. Actually the "spiritual" of the shoutin' congregation has more in common with hot jazz than it has with the "spiritual" sung by the highbrow Negro concert singer. And the carefully and deliberately arranged and notated "spiritual," which is made the subject of "interpretations," is in some ways more akin to certain varieties of "sweet" jazz than it is to the spontaneous outpouring of religious emotion peculiar to the naïve rural Negro by whom all true spirituals are originally conceived. The need of another classification for musical purposes is obvious, one based on differ-

47

ences in form, technique and method of creation, rather than differences in social function or in the character of accompanying texts.

Certain rough distinctions are obvious. The least European, hence the most purely Negroid, variety of Afro-American music is to be found in the embryonic spiritual of the shoutin' congregation. It is less standardized in pattern, more varied in style, freer in form than the hottest of hot jazz. A comparison with African tribal music will show it to be related to its jungle prototypes. Hot jazz, on the other hand, exhibits the influences of sophisticated city life, and something of the standardization usually associated with commercial products. The mere fact that hot jazz is played upon complex standardized instruments of European origin (the influence of the piano keyboard is particularly important in this connection) gives it a sophisticated character totally lacking in the shoutin' spiritual. The human voice, feet and hands are instruments common to both the American and the African Negro; the piano, trumpet, silver-plated banjo and saxophone are not.

Nevertheless, hot jazz and the shoutin' spiritual are in certain respects remarkably similar. Both are largely improvisatory. Both are Negroid in their participative, rather than artist-audience, approach. Both are far richer in purely Negroid rhythmic and scalar elements than are the more deliberate forms of jazz or of Afro-American religious music.

The term "hot" is, however, a relative one. Much of the music which it commonly designates is only partially improvised. Both in the religious and in the jazz fields, particularly pleasing improvisations are apt to be remembered and repeated more or less intact, to be accorded something of the status of "compositions." Here we have, perhaps, another, though a closely related, variety of Negroid music, slightly more deliberate and clearly crystallized than the purely improvised variety, but still showing most of the traits of Negroid improvisation. Most of what is popularly known (even among swing enthusiasts) as "hot jazz" belongs to this category of remembered and repeated, partially rehearsed, music.

Commercial recordings of purely improvisatory shoutin' music are, as far as I know, absolutely non-existent. From time to time, however, records do appear that approximate the authentic style of our second (remembered and repeated) category. A now disbanded vocal quartet known as Mitchell's Christian Singers recorded for Melotone about a decade ago several spirituals that contain rich stores of characteristic Negro elements. These spirituals (*What More Can Jesus Do?*, *Who Was John?*, etc.) are obviously somewhat rehearsed and polished, but they exhibit many features that are not even remotely expressible in musical notation. Like most types of Negro music that attain momentary popularity, the Mitchell's Christian Singers' style was widely imitated and ultimately commercialized. The Golden Gate Quartet, another Negro ensemble, continued the tradition for a time, and it ultimately reached wide radio success at the hands of a group called the Ink Spots. But though more successful, none of these Negro singing ensembles quite repeated the musical subtlety and primitive sincerity recorded on the original Mitchell's Christian Singers' discs.

Recordings of analogous music in the field of jazz are common enough. The better recordings of such musicians as Duke Ellington, Bessie Smith, Louis Armstrong, Fats Waller, Benny Goodman and the orchestra of Fletcher Henderson may be said to conform roughly to the peculiarities of our "remem-

49

bered and repeated" category. They, like the Mitchell's Christian Singers' records, are to a certain extent improvisatory, completely devoid of the stiffening effort to reproduce written notes in sound, and yet are obviously somewhat rehearsed and deliberate. Most "swing music" so called belongs to this category. So far we have been speaking of hot jazz and of what, by analogy, we may term the "hot" spiritual.

From here to the next category is a long jump, though the intervening boundary is overlapped here and there by musical works of special character. Here the printed page begins to be felt as an influence. Rehearsal and performance of "interpretations" before passive audiences come into the picture. The man who writes music, as opposed to the man who plays it, achieves some prominence. The spiritual and the jazz piece alike become "compositions." At this point also a type of music that may be quite accurately described as pseudo-Negroid and that is at the same time almost indistinguishable from published music of true Negro origins begins to appear. In drawing these distinctions the writer does not mean to imply that the music of one category is superior or inferior to that of another. The main scope of the present volume is analytical rather than critical. There is much noble and truly inspired music to be found in the published collections of "concert" spirituals; there is some clever writing to be discerned in the compositions and arrangements of Tin Pan Alley and the "sweet" dance orchestrators. Again the religious expression shows far more depth and variety than does the secular. But both these types of music are far removed, musically speaking, from the elemental manifestations of the Negro idiom as we find them in the shoutin' spiritual.

The great bulk of the recorded and published spirituals

belong, in the form that we know them, to the category I have designated as that of the "concert" spiritual. Most of them derive, either wholly or partly from "hot" sources, but they are now fixed compositions, and, as such, profoundly different both aesthetically and technically from the Negroid expressions of which they are the outgrowth. *Swing Low, Sweet Chariot* is now a traditional melody in the white man's sense, and may be written down, harmonized and played according to the rules of his musical art. That original *Swing Low, Sweet Chariot* that crystallized "hot" from the ripe emotions of some now forgotten group of rural Negro worshippers, was undoubtedly a very different musical experience. Some of the published spirituals are unquestionably truer to Negroid sources than others. Some are notational approximations of impressions from shoutin' services. Some have been taken down from the "posed" performance of Negroes who take part regularly in such services. Some, perhaps a majority, have been notated from the singing of the more polished, rehearsed and artistically conscious Negro choruses which, from the days of the Fiske Jubilee Singers to those of the Hall Johnson, Tuskegee and Hampton Choirs, have been making a valued contribution to concert music. Still others have been detached completely from their original settings, provided with piano accompaniments, and placed, in this completely transcribed form, at the disposal of the maker of miscellaneous concert programs. Here, even though the interpreter be a Negro, we have a composition that is far more white than Negroid. When Roland Hayes, Paul Robeson or Marian Anderson sings a group of spirituals on a program in Carnegie Hall, the result may be a moving musical experience, but the music itself is likely to be only superficially Negroid in character.

JAZZ: HOT AND HYBRID

Returning to the corresponding category of jazz—that of the published, rehearsed and performed "composition"—we are confronted with a bewildering idiomatic mixture. Tin Pan Alley, prolific source of virtually all of America's published popular music, has for half a century been located in what is America's most cosmopolitan, and in many ways least American, city. Its creations reflect a dozen different musical backgrounds. Some of its output is pseudo-Negroid in character; but a surprising amount of it has no relation whatever to the Afro-American idiom or to jazz. On the other hand there is the tradition of sophisticated jazz performance—of the "sweet" dance orchestra—a wholly American phenomenon seemingly of Western and Middle Western origins which has filled an intermediate function between Tin Pan Alley and the public. Much of Tin Pan Alley's output that is not jazz has become jazz through performance by jazz bands. Such song hits of the World War I repertoire as *Whispering, Smiles* and *Trail of the Lonesome Pine* were no more jazz than is that item whose cheerful mutilation by jazz bands was popular during the same period, Rimsky-Korsakoff's *Song of India.* The Anglo-Celtic ballad style has had, and still holds, a predominant influence in American popular music, and it is closely seconded in influence by the Paris-Vienna operetta tradition. Neither of these types of music bears intrinsically the remotest relation to jazz. The list of Tin Pan Alley compositions that are wholly, or almost wholly devoid of jazz influence would be one of tremendous length and would, I suspect, include a large majority of the "hits." Suffice it to recall that such tremendous best-sellers as Al Bryan's *Joan of Arc,* Harry Akst's *Baby Face* and the Whiting-Donaldson *My Blue Heaven*; such widely howled bits of musical claptrap as *Yes, We Have No*

CLASSIFICATIONS AND DEFINITIONS

Bananas, Sing Something Simple and *Christopher Columbus*; and such truly beautiful compositions as Jerome Kern's *Smoke Gets in Your Eyes* are among the number. And we have not mentioned here anything from the category of the waltz, a category that has always held its place in the public favor (think of the enormous sales of *Ramona, I'm Forever Blowing Bubbles, Pagan Love Song*), and that is wholly foreign to the jazz idiom.

It is, however, from the field of Tin Pan Alley's largely non-jazz expression that the "sweet" jazz artists, from Art Hickman to Guy Lombardo, have drawn the melodies on which their particular art has been based. And this art, one with definable elements of Negro origin, is unquestionably a variety of jazz, a hybrid variety that has come about as close as anything does to being the folk-music of the great mass of Americans. *Baby Face, Whispering* and *Smoke Gets in Your Eyes* may not be jazz melodies in their published form, but in the form in which the American knows and remembers them—in the form, that is, in which they have been played by countless orchestras from one end of the country to the other—they are jazz.

Tin Pan Alley's creative activity has not, on the other hand, been uninfluenced by the Negro idiom. A certain portion of its output has, from the days of the minstrel shows, shown the traces, in harmonic clichés and melodic patterns, of the Negro method of performance. Some of this music has been straightforwardly pseudo-Negroid or "blackface," with texts in Negro dialect. Some of it has been the genuine work of Negro composers. Some has been Negroid only in the melodic structure of a phrase or two. In isolated cases—compositions like Gershwin's *Fascinating Rhythm* and the trick piano works of Zez

53

Confrey—Negroid habits of melodic thought have been reduced to formulas which in turn have been elaborated for more sophisticated purposes. The stock-in-trade piano accompaniments provided by the Tin Pan Alley publishers for their sheet music versions usually exhibit two or three well-worn Negroid rhythmic patterns. It is only natural that the methods of syncopation used by the average "sweet" orchestra should make their way back to the composers of the tunes employed by such orchestras, and that they should reappear in printed form in the work of these composers. Thus, Tin Pan Alley composes some music that is influenced by jazz idioms, some that is not. In the end, in terms of performance, virtually all of it except the waltzes becomes jazz.

Small differences aside, then, we have distinguished for our present purposes two general types of jazz, both of which represent types of *performance* rather than types of *composition*. They are "hot" jazz and "sweet" or commercial jazz. The former is more purely Negroid, more purely improvisatory, and comparatively independent of composed "tunes." The latter is the dance and amusement music of the American people as a whole. The tunes on which it is based issue from Tin Pan Alley, the center of the popular song-publishing industry. These tunes are, some of them, purely Anglo-Celtic or Central European in character, some of them pseudo-Negroid.

Chapter 4

ELEMENTARY RHYTHMIC FORMULAS

IT HAS BEEN pointed out by writers on the subject that jazz rhythm is characterized by two distinct structural devices which are uncommon, or less common, in other types of music. These are: (1) simple syncopation and (2) the peculiar superimposition of conflicting rhythms known as "secondary rag" or "polyrhythm." The first of these has been traced, rightly or wrongly, to European sources, and is supposed to be based on an old and well-known formula of classical composition. It is commonly thought to have been the basis of ragtime as distinct from jazz, the latter type of music involving polyrhythm as well as syncopation. The second device—polyrhythm—has been heralded as the true Negro contribution, and as the fundamental and distinguishing element of jazz rhythm.

Simple syncopation is a common enough device to be familiar to anyone with a slight acquaintance with music. Grove's *Dictionary of Music and Musicians* defines it as "an alteration of regular rhythm, produced by placing the strongest emphasis on part of the bar not usually accented." Essentially it is the upsetting of a normal rhythmic pulse by the appearance of a stress on a weak beat while the following strong beat is deprived of such stress. In its most elementary form it is represented by a quarter note followed by a half note in an ordinary bar of four-quarter time. Here, where the normal, regular stresses of four-quarter time would fall upon the first and third beats of the bar ($\frac{4}{4}$ ♩♩|♩♩) one finds the stresses shifted to the first and second beats ($\frac{4}{4}$♩♩𝄽). With the second beat the element of syncopation enters, and the regular pulse is destroyed.

This elementary germ of syncopation may be extended until a definable *counter rhythm* is set up: $\frac{4}{4}$ ♩♩♩♩♩|♩ in this case a rhythm of units equal to those of the normal rhythm. A syncopation often gives the impression of anticipating a normal beat, as the ear tends to expect a normal one, and accepts the appearance of the abnormal one as its hurried or advanced representative. When one establishes a regular pulse $\frac{4}{4}$ ♩♩|♩♩ and then introduces a syncopation $\frac{4}{4}$ ♩♩𝄽 the ear is likely to take the syncopated note for a regular pulse that has gotten misplaced. Syncopation may thus be used as a means of rhythmic distortion—as a method of achieving surprise—and this is one of its common functions in jazz.

It will be noted that there are two processes involved in the creation of syncopation. First, the establishment of a regular or normal rhythm; second, the creation of an abnormal deviation from this rhythm. These processes may occur simultaneously in the interplay of two different rhythmic voices, or they may occur in a single rhythmic voice where the normal rhythm is first indicated and fixed in the memory and the abnormal deviation follows. In the first case the contrast is achieved directly—the syncopated voice standing out in relief against a regularly pulsating background:

 In the second, the background is first established and the deviation arrives to break up what would otherwise be its logical continuation: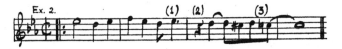

The normal recurrence of a musical element may be either anticipated or delayed by syncopation. Both anticipative and retardative syncopation are found in jazz though the former device is perhaps the commoner. The familiar phrase of *Whispering*

Example 1.

for example, was often found in jazz-band performances of its period as

Ex. 2.

The deviation from the normal here is complicated by other elements besides those of simple syncopation, but the example contains two anticipative syncopations (at (1) and (3) respectively) and one retardative syncopation (at (2)).

The anticipation or delaying of an element may be by a considerable time value or by a very slight one. Anticipations of long notes by small fractions of their values (in performance sometimes the fractions turn out to be nearly infinitesimal) are quite common. The curious reader is referred among countless examples to the trumpet solo at the beginning of Louis Armstrong's recording of the *Mahogany Hall Stomp* (Vocalion 3055) as a particularly effective use of slight anticipations which are too small and indefinite to be conveyed in notational terms but which are part and parcel of the infectious "swing" that the recording possesses.

Any page of sheet-music jazz will reveal a number of common simple syncopative formulas applied to melodic purposes. The bass part will usually mark the normal rhythm in straight invariable pulses, while the right hand part will syncopate now and then against it—anticipating its beats or their regular subdivisions by various fractions of their value. Here and there the bass part may itself become syncopative, or may leave off for a few beats while the right-hand part syncopates for the moment without the contrasting background of regularity. In such cases we have what we might call "internal" syncopation based on the memory of an established pulse rather than on direct contrast with a simultaneous rhythmic voice.

Performance of the music by any competent jazz pianist or orchestra will reveal a great many more complications of simple syncopation than appear on the printed page. The use of the device (when not specifically indicated in the printed version) is an important part of the technique of rhythmic distortion known as "jazzing," or more recently as "swinging."

*   *   *   *   *

The second basic syncopative device of jazz consists in the superimposition of a rhythm of different phrase-lengths, but of identical metric units, upon the prevailing rhythm of the music. Usually the superimposed rhythm falls into phrases of three units which are set against a background of the nor-

mal four-quarter rhythm of jazz. The device, in its simplest
form, is illustrated by the following examples:

It has nothing in common, despite a superficial similarity
of ideas and some misinformed writing on the subject, with
the "two-against-three" or "three-against-four" devices so common in the music of classical European composers. In the
latter there is no disturbance of normal rhythm. Strong beats
remain strong beats. The lengths of the note-groups are the
same and the metrical units comprising them differ. In the
rhythmic superimpositions of jazz, however, there is real syncopation resulting from the displacement of accents from strong
to weak beats.

Don Knowlton, in what has become possibly the most
quoted article on the subject of jazz, was probably the first
person to draw attention in clearly defined terms to this peculiarity of its rhythm. Knowlton's article, *The Anatomy of Jazz*,
appeared in the April 1926 issue of *Harper's*. Before him
the late Henry Edward Krehbiel had hinted at the polyrhythmic character of Negro music. In the *Musical Courier*
for June 1, 1922, the Negro musicologist, Nicholas J. G.
Ballanta-Taylor, had quoted examples of this type of rhythmic structure and noted that it was peculiar to jazz and other
Negro musical expression. Knowlton, however, was appar-

ently the first to isolate this germ of jazz and to point out that, reduced to a simple formula, it formed one of the basic devices of the Tin Pan Alley jazz composer.

Knowlton defines the peculiarity as "the imposition of a *one*, two, three element in rhythm upon the one, two, three, four fundamental." He continues: "This, I believe, is the only characteristic of jazz which is truly of American—or rather, of Afro-American—origin.

"A Negro guitar-player once asked me, 'You know the difference between primary rag and secondary rag?'

"His primary rag was simple syncopation; his secondary rag was this superimposition of *one*, two, three upon the basic one, two, three, four.·

"Graphically, it may be expressed thus:

1	2	3	1	2	3	1	2	3	1	2	3	1	2	3	1
1		2		3		4		1		2		3		4	

"Although originally presented in the melody as in the *Down Home Rag* (see musical score) and sometimes accentuated there even today, as in *Kitten on the Keys*, the idea rapidly shifted from melody into accompaniment and, as it is a rhythmic rather than a melodic principle, it has found its exponents principally in the banjo and the drum. . . . The Negro guitar-player was right . . . it is a 'secondary rag.' And it is this subsidiary *one*, two, three on top of the underlying tempo that makes shoulder-muscles twitch, that bedevils hips, that provokes wiggles and twists on the dance floor, and causes blue-noses to cry out that jazz is a great immoral influence."

The example from the *Down Home Rag* which Knowlton quotes is the following:

ELEMENTARY RHYTHMIC FORMULAS

(The explanatory brackets are the present writer's.) There is also a quotation from Confrey's *Kitten on the Keys* which we shall consider presently.

In Knowlton's remarks the New York composer Aaron Copland found the basis for a broader theoretical principle which he outlined in an article in *Modern Music*, for January 1927, under the term "polyrhythm." Copland found the current method of notating "secondary rag" passages misleading. He pointed out that the common notation of the phenomenon was an over-simplification of what in reality was a pair of contrasting metrical "voices." The rhythm $\frac{4}{4}$ ♫♫♩♫♫♩ , common in jazz as well as in such Latin-American Negroid products as the tango, should properly be written $\frac{3}{8}$ ♫♫ | ♩ ♪ | $\frac{2}{8}$ ♫ . The elementary principle of "secondary rag" was, according to Copland, something hitherto foreign to Western music: the interplay of two or more different rhythms. Over the normal four-quarter rhythm of jazz one actually had a rhythmic voice whose phrases were not phrases of four-quarter time at all. He also gave the principle a somewhat wider application (though one unevenly supported in purely Negroid music) by noting that "polyrhythm" could be, and was by certain Tin-Pan-Alleyites,

61

applied in many other ways—ways involving other phrase groups than those of three units in the superimposed rhythm. Theoretically the principle had immense possibilities, since the number of different superimpositions was limited only by the infinities of mathematics. Some of these were exploited by Gershwin (*Fascinating Rhythm*) and by Copland himself in extended symphonic compositions. But the vast bulk of commercial jazz continued to follow the unelaborated three-over-four superimposition to which the Southern Negro had also apparently given his preference.

It was Copland's contention that "polyrhythm" and syncopation were two different things. In fact, Copland's words on the subject were later interpreted by the late Isaac Goldberg (*Tin Pan Alley*,[1] p. 274) as meaning that "we may have jazz without any syncopation." The question is, perhaps, merely a matter of definition, and a complete and accurate definition of the word "syncopation" has always been difficult to arrive at. There is certainly an important difference between "secondary rag" and what I have termed simple syncopation; but the principle of polyrhythm would seem, none the less, to be a syncopative principle. Copland defines polyrhythm as "a play of two independent rhythms." Now, syncopation in any extended form also constitutes a "play of two independent rhythms," inasmuch as a different system of accent is set up against a normal system. The simple syncopation $\frac{4}{4}$ may be considered as such a rhythmic "play"; a fact that is brought out more clearly in the

[1] Published by The John Day Company, New York, 1930.

ELEMENTARY RHYTHMIC FORMULAS

following notation of it:

$$\frac{4}{4}\ \text{♩}\ |\ \text{♩}\ \ \text{♩}\ |\ \text{♩}\ \ \text{♩}\ |$$

$$\frac{4}{4}\ \text{♩}\ \ \text{♩}\ |\ \text{♩}\ \ \text{♩}\ |$$

Here, however, the accents of the superimposed rhythm are spaced similarly to those of the basic rhythm (*i.e.* a half note apart). In the "secondary rag" type of syncopation on the

other hand $\frac{4}{4}$ the accents of the superim-

posed rhythm are spaced differently from those of the basic rhythm (*i.e.* three quarter notes apart). This would appear to be the fundamental difference between extended simple syncopation and polyrhythmic syncopation. It is, at any rate, convenient to have a term for the latter phenomenon, and polyrhythm is perhaps as good as any.

Polyrhythm, then—in its elementary three-over-four superimposition—is found in a host of phraseological variations in most ordinary sheet-music jazz. Here it is most commonly defined by melodic contour. The perfect simple example is to be found in the melody of the Fields-McHugh song *I Can't Give You Anything but Love, Baby* (1928):

Ex.4.

etc. A more complicated example is provided in Zez Confrey's *Kitten on the Keys:*

63

It is also found in many less explicit forms, as in the very common melodic rhythms of *Walking My Baby Back Home* where rhythmic groups of three are loosely indicated in the melodic physiognomy:

In the rhythm of the Charleston ($\frac{4}{4}$ ♩. ♪♩), and elsewhere,

it affects accompaniment as well as melody.

To sum up: the basic rhythmic characteristics of ordinary printed sheet-music jazz are two varieties of syncopation, (1) simple syncopation and (2) the polyrhythmic superimposition of three-over-four. To trace the origins of the latter phenomenon, its various melodic and harmonic ramifications in actual performance, and its relation to the Afro-American musical idiom will be the task of succeeding chapters.

Chapter 5

ANATOMY OF JAZZ MELODY

WHILE POLYRHYTHM is a basic ingredient of all jazz, it seldom shows itself in mathematically precise patterns. Most jazz melodies exhibit polyrhythmic peculiarities. An underlying feeling of polyrhythmic accent affects their phraseology, and gives it a characteristic stamp. But the naked formula of three superimposed on four is something that is usually implied rather than stated.

Certain trick compositions by such writers as Zez Confrey do contain measures and measures of exact polyrhythm. His *Kitten on the Keys* and *Stumbling* are cases in point. But these are sophisticated works by a composer who has used the formula consciously. In the general run of jazz melodies, whether hot or hybrid, polyrhythmic elements are less mathematical, freer and more subtle. Here it is often merely some peculiarity of accent or of the rhythmic behavior of certain isolated tones that betrays the presence of polyrhythm. Sometimes it is difficult to track down the distinguishing feature. Often polyrhythm and simple syncopation offer themselves as alternative explanations of a given phraseological quirk. Often it is hard to say which is involved.· But the three-over-four superimposition does turn up with remarkable consistency in the melodies of Afro-American music.

It is quite a jump from the explicit polyrhythm of the first two measures of *I Can't Give you Anything but Love, Baby* to the following well-known phrase from Arthur L. Schwartz's *Dancing in the Dark:*

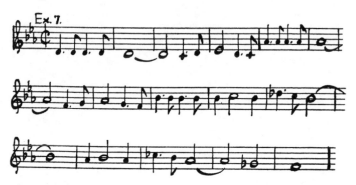

Yet when we examine the latter melody (taken at random from among dozens of similar sweet jazz tunes) we find that it contains unmistakable evidence, in the last eight bars, of polyrhythmic structure. Notice, for example, the behavior of the note B flat in the ninth, tenth and eleventh bars. It enters on the first and third beats of the measure, establishing itself as a normally repeated pulse. Then it begins to appear at syncopated intervals, upsetting the regularity previously established. Measure the distances between its syncopated appearances in measures ten and eleven and you will find that it is now being sounded at intervals of three units. The same thing occurs with the note A flat in the thirteenth and fourteenth bars. Following an initial establishment of the normal pulse, we have in each case a polyrhythmic pattern (our old friend three-over-four). And this time the polyrhythmic pattern is defined not by the whole melodic contour but by the recurrence of a single element. The example will be made clearer, perhaps, if we omit from bars nine to fourteen all notes except the B flat and the A flat and replace them with rests:

ANATOMY OF JAZZ MELODY

It is the appearance of such rhythmo-melodic peculiarities as this that stamps a tune like *Dancing in the Dark* as unmistakably Afro-American.[1]

Sometimes polyrhythm is defined, as above, by the repetition of a certain melodic tone. At others it will be found defined only by the relative length of the notes composing a phrase. An example of this is to be found in the following little phrase which has cropped up incessantly in jazz melodies during the past twenty years: . The importance of note No. 3 in this example is attested not only by its length, but also by the fact that it is usually a note of the prevailing harmony where 1 and 2 are apt to be non-chordic (*i.e.* what the harmony books call appoggiaturas or passing tones). How often has the melody of the already quoted Fields-McHugh song been distorted in performance as follows:

[1] The reader will note that the terms *Afro-American* and *Negroid* are used throughout the present work to describe musical peculiarities that can be traced to Negro sources. The terms are used without reference to the race of the composer or player whose music is quoted. Much of America's Negroid music is actually written and played by whites, but it is none the less Afro-American in style.

The pattern is the same. It will be found in a rather mechanical form in the incessant rhythm of that optimistic hymn *Happy Days Are Here Again*

etc., ad nauseam. Here it does not appear exclusively at the phrase endings but is used continuously and with relentless unimaginativeness.

A related pattern is the ♩. ♪♩♩ ♩ rhythm found in the second and third measures of

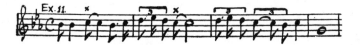

In both this and the last previously mentioned pattern there may legitimately be some doubt as to whether the rhythm is essentially polyrhythmic or whether it represents merely a syncopated (simple) advancement of the third unit of the bar. Whether, in symbols, there is a feeling of a genuine three-over-four disturbance (♩♪♪♩ | or ♫♩ ♪♩ |) or whether, for example, ♩ ♫♩ is merely a distortion of ♩ ♩ ♩ The question probably cannot be definitely settled, and in any case it is only a theoretical one. The fact remains that the third beat of the $\frac{4}{4}$ bar is often anticipated in jazz melodies by an eighth note.

Lying similarly in a doubtful penumbra between poly-

rhythm and simple syncopation are such melodies as the following:

and

Here an examination of repeated notes will not reveal the
definite polyrhythmic formula implied in melodies like *Dancing in the Dark.* In each case, however, the highest note is introduced first on strong beats, and then on that particular off-
beat (before the 3rd beat of the measure) so beloved of the
jazz song writer. One can, of course, detect a suspicion of
polyrhythm in the contour of measure 2 of each where the
metrical accent after the bar-line and the melodic accent on
the last half (or quarter) of the second beat define a group
of three

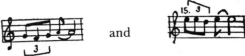

Polyrhythmic or not, these melodies belong to a type of jazz
tune that is very common. The type is distinguished by the
peculiar behavior of the note that is struck on the third beat of
the first measure. It repeats itself every time exactly $3\frac{1}{2}$ beats
later on the last half of the second beat of the second measure.

There is one point of similarity between this rhythmic
peculiarity and the more clearly defined type of polyrhythm.

Both depend for their effect, like all syncopations, on the relation between the strong and the weak beats of musical metre.

The musical measure (to repeat an axiom of elementary theory) consists of a number of beats, of which some are stronger than others. In normal   time the first is the most powerful, the third is next in order of rank, and the second and fourth are weaker. If the measure is subdivided into eighth-note values a new set of subordinate beats is added. The first and third beats retain their supremacy, the second and fourth become lesser dignitaries, and the eighths constituting the last half of each beat become the weakest units of the series.  This accentual relationship is fundamental to the metre of music as we know it.

Now syncopation, as we have already seen, results in the temporary disturbance of this normal order of accentual precedence. Polyrhythm of three over four entails its own particular type of disturbance. If a polyrhythmic cycle of three starts on a strong beat (   ) the next cyclical accent will fall on a weak one (   ) and a disruption of normal rhythm will result. A similar disruption occurs in the rhythm indicated by the melodic contour of the example quoted above. An important note is heard on the third beat of the first measure, a beat of considerable strength. The next appearance of the note is on a weak beat—the third eighth of the following measure:

And this beat is very weak indeed, being the subordinate of a beat (the second of the measure) that is already weak among the measure's accentual subalterns.

The relation between the strong and weak beats of musical metre has, of course, always exercised an effect on the contour of European melody. In jazz, because of the importance of syncopated elements, the effect is peculiar and in some ways more pronounced. The jazz musician has a remarkable sense of subdivided and subordinate accents in what he is playing, even though it be the slowest sort of jazz. This awareness of minute component metrical units shows itself in all sorts of syncopative subtleties that are quite foreign to European music. It is, I think, the lack of this awareness in most European "classical" musicians that explains their well-known inability to play jazz in a convincing manner.

As to the syncopative subtleties of the hot jazz improviser more will be said in due course. We are still concerned here with such simple, elementary patterns as are the stock-in-trade of the average commercial jazz composer, arranger or player.

*   *   *   *   *

An interesting feature of jazz melody lies in the various expedients used by the player and the jazz composer to intensify the distinction between the strong and weak beats of the measure. The most obvious of these is, of course, that of simply accenting the strong beats (𝄴 ♪♪♪♪ ♪♪♪♪). Another method of defining the normal metrical accent of the strong beats is through the movement of the melodic con-

71

tour. A third and very characteristic method is to give the strong beats notes of greater, and the weak beats notes of lesser, value. This method, which is characteristic of a vast amount of popular Tin Pan Alley writing, results in a skip-

ping, long-short-long-short rhythm () which has

been referred to by Don Knowlton under the alluring term "umpateedle."

Now "umpateedle" rhythm is not in itself a novel or un-usual phenomenon. It has been used often in virtually every variety of folk and concert music from the classical gigue to such popular Latin tunes as *Valencia*, and from Haydn to Mahler. Its principal interest in connection with jazz rhythm lies in its power of intensifying the normal accents of the measure so that they may serve as a. more striking back-ground for subsequent or simultaneous rhythmic distortion. Among its functions is that of exaggerating the normal pulse so that the polyrhythmic or other syncopative patterns of a melody may stand out in higher relief. When a melodic

figure in straight eighths

is changed to one of "umpateedle" character

the dotted eighths, by their increased value, give a feeling of greater weight to the normal rhythm of the measure, en-trenching the solid metrical pulse even more firmly than before. When, subsequently, the melody moves to an aber-ration from the normal rhythm as it does at *a*:

the effect is more striking than it would have been had the
first figure consisted of plain eighth-notes.

Similarly, in the following example (from *Someday Sweetheart* as recorded by the Benny Goodman Trio, Victor
25181-A), the effect of the syncopation at *b* is all the stronger
since the weak beat on which it occurs is rendered even weaker
by the shortness of the note that represents it.

One need only compare this example with its straight eighth
equivalent

to appreciate this fact.

The entrance of the syncopation is on a weak beat (the
eighth eighth of the bar) even in the straight eighth version.
In the "umpateedle" version the point of its entrance has
been shifted to the bar's sixteenth sixteenth, which belongs to
a still lower category in the system of accentual precedence.
For if we divide a measure into sixteenth-note values

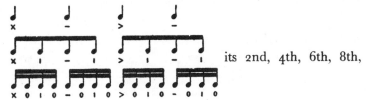

its 2nd, 4th, 6th, 8th,

73

10th, 12th, 14th and 16th sixteenths (indicated by o's) are weaker than even the weakest of the remaining sixteenths which correspond to eighth-note pulses. A syncopation, or syncopative accent, is striking in direct proportion to the weakness of the metric beat on which it enters. Hence the effect, through "umpateedle," has been intensified.

Where the simultaneous rhythmic relationships of poly-rhythm enter into the question, the "umpateedle" formula performs even more striking services. When a polyrhythmic pattern expressed in straight eighth-notes

is converted into "umpateedle" rhythm a curious thing oc-curs. The polyrhythmic distortion is itself distorted by the fundamental rhythm. Its successive cycles become alternately

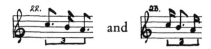

depending on whether or not they commence on an accented beat of the fundamental rhythm. While the melodic contour still falls into groups of three, the relation of the note values indicates the fundamental four-quarter metre. And thus in a single voice, without help from any accompaniment, we have, clearly defined, the conflict of rhythmic stresses that constitutes polyrhythm:

ANATOMY OF JAZZ MELODY

The melody of the *Down Home Rag* quoted from Don Knowlton's article is a simple and mathematically perfect example of this formula. There are many others. The best known example is, of course, Confrey's *Kitten on the Keys*. One need only reduce the "umpateedle" rhythm of the latter composition to straight eighths

to appreciate how much its character depends on the redistortions of the dotted eighth rhythm. Confrey's polyrhythmic pattern here incidentally contains another defining element (the use of doubled notes on the first two beats of each polyrhythmic cycle) that helps to re-assert the precedence of the distorted polyrhythm over the fundamental rhythm that has distorted it. The whole composition offers a remarkable interplay of rhythmic distortions and distortions of distortions. Two conflicting rhythms are continuously pulling at its melodic structure, neither of them gaining complete control of it. The "umpateedle" rhythm lends its powerful support to the fundamental pulse of the measure, its influence mutilating the superimposed cycles of the counter-rhythm. And the scars it inflicts on the superimposed cycles emphasize further their syncopative, or polyrhythmic, character.

Now the "umpateedle" rhythm, as jazz composers and players continually use it, is not necessarily a fundamental or integral ingredient of jazz melody. It may be merely an optional embellishment. Melodies originally written in straight eighths are not altered by conversion from straight eighths to "umpateedle." The ear accepts the original effects of syncopation even when they have been distorted by the introduction of dotted eighths and sixteenths. When the

pattern 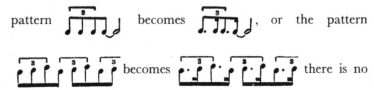 becomes , or the pattern

becomes there is no

alteration in the character of the polyrhythmic superimpositions of three, even though the note values comprising them may be altered considerably. They still remain polyrhythmic, and analyzable as such. The effect is merely that of intensifying the strong, as opposed to the weak, beats of the fundamental rhythm.

The question may have occurred to the reader whether the influence of the "umpateedle" rhythm is invariably thrown to the support of the fundamental pulse, or whether, on the other hand, it may also be used to intensify the superimposed cycles of a polyrhythmic passage. That it can be so used is obvious. Examples of its use in the latter manner are infrequent however. The present writer cannot locate, offhand, any instance of it in printed jazz, though such instances probably exist. In performance one comes across it occasionally in the playing of a jazz band of unusually acute rhythmic sense. In default of examples, we can create one of our own. The simple cycles of *I Can't Give You Anything but Love* offer a clear basis for "umpateedle" intensification. One result might be:

ANATOMY OF JAZZ MELODY

The Fields-McHugh ode to love and poverty has undoubtedly received this sort of treatment occasionally from one or the other of the more wide-awake dance ensembles.

"Umpateedle" rhythm is commonly associated with the slower types of jazz where its rhythmic subdivisions of the eighth-note find room for comfortable articulation. It is seldom to be found in the hectic rhythms of the faster fox-trots.

In actual performance the dotted eighth and sixteenth of the printed "umpateedle" usually turn out to be more in the nature of a triplet eighth and sixteenth. ♫♫ , that is, appears as an easy ♪♪♪♪. This is so consistently the case that one suspects the usual notation of it to be an inaccurate simplification of what is intended. Further confirmation of the triplet nature of "umpateedle" rhythm is to be found in the large number of instances in hot improvised solos where "umpateedle" patterns are continually interspersed with actual three-note triplets. Examples are to be found on every hand.[2] A clarinet break at the conclusion of *Someday Sweetheart* as recorded by the Benny Goodman Trio (Victor 25181-A), offers a convenient one:

As the faster tempos of jazz are approached the "umpateedle" rhythm is more apt to be replaced by straight eighths

[2] The "umpateedle" triplet is likewise found in published spirituals. See, for example, *You Goin' To Reap Jus' What You Sow* (p. 28 in *Religious Folk-Songs of the Negro*, Hampton Institute Press, 1927).

and the rhythmic stress of the strong beats to be conveyed by accent rather than by difference in note values. The precise point where "umpateedle" slips over into ♪ ♩ ♩ ♪ ♩ is difficult to define. Those interested will find in the Benny Goodman Trio recording of *Who?* (Victor 25181-B) a number of clarinet passages that seem to waver unclassifiably between a broad, almost even, "umpateedle" and a definite series of alternately accented straight eighths.

*   *   *   *   *

Among the other more obvious peculiarities of jazz melody the distortion of repeated phrases deserves a passing note. This again rests upon the syncopative shifting of corresponding elements from strong to weak beats. Something has been said in the previous chapter about the syncopative distortion of printed melodies in actual performance. There is a large number of jazz melodies in which a somewhat similar type of distortion forms an essential part of the original melodic structure. The well-known motif of *Limehouse Blues* is a case in point:

Ex. 29.

Here the melodic pattern formed by the first three notes is repeated in a syncopated distortion, each of its notes being shifted to a weak beat and the length of the pattern being stretched to five instead of the original three eighths. In the following measure the pattern again assumes its normal aspect. Here polyrhythm also happens to be involved, the pattern itself (in its original form) constituting a superimposed cycle of three. A very simple example involving only two notes is to be found in the characteristic phrase from Handy's *Ole Miss Blues:*

I just want to tell you this—

Handy's *The Basement Blues* contains an interesting pair of measures in which the repeated phrase appears successively in three different forms:

Ev-ry day I get low as a toad

The rhythmic effect of these distortions is always catchy. Like the jazz composer's polyrhythmic tricks, they are usually simple formulas generalized from the more spontaneous out-pourings of Negro musicians.

*   *   *   *   *

In closing a word might be said about that common rhythmic formula of European music, the famous "two against three" which constitutes a proverbial worry of the young piano student. While by no means the most characteristic feature of jazz rhythm, it does occasionally appear even in hot improvisation.[3] At the hands of the Tin Pan Alley "sweet" arrangers it has become one more stock-in-trade pattern to be used ad nauseam. In hot jazz, except where it forms an outgrowth of the "umpateedle" rhythm as in the above example from *Someday Sweetheart* (Goodman), its ap-

[3] It occurs also occasionally in the published spirituals. See *Religious Folk-Songs of the Negro,* Hampton Institute Press, p. 28, p. 40.

pearance seems to be incidental. Duke Ellington's early recordings contain an occasional triplet of extended value and
they are to be met with here and there in the bulk of hot
recordings. More often however, what appears at first hear-

ing to be a triplet (♩ ♩ ♩) is actually a sort of pseudo triplet
        3

formed by syncopation or by a combination of small polyrhythmic units

The latter type of polyrhythmic formation, which is both more
subtle and more characteristically Negroid than the triplet,
will be considered in another connection further on.

Chapter 6

HOT RHYTHM

MUSIC IS INSEPARABLE from human emotion, and its forms are dictated by psychologic rather than mathematical considerations. The Negro did not invent the peculiar concept of polyrhythm and then proceed to embody it in his music. None but the most musically sophisticated members of the race are conscious of the formulas that stamp Negro music as a characteristic form of expression. Those who create it most successfully are the ones who know least about its abstract structure. The Negro, like all folk musicians, expresses himself intuitively. The geometric patterns which the theorist later discerns as peculiar to his type of music are generalizations, and, like all generalizations, they are simplified symbols which seldom coincide perfectly with reality.

The leaves of a plant may be described as triangular. Yet no two of them will be precisely alike, nor will any one of them—except perhaps accidentally—conform to the dimensions of a geometrically perfect triangle. Nevertheless, in a rough way there will be a certain conformity to the triangular idea, and the symbol of the triangle provides the analytical mind with a useful means of identifying the plant and of classifying it among other types of vegetation. A somewhat similar situation presents itself in the analysis of musical form. Neither the Negro folk musician nor the plant is consciously attempting to fulfill a geometric destiny. Nor do either of their efflorescences often coincide perfectly with the analyst's theoretical machinery. But the earmarks of his abstract patterns do crop up in various ways even though the patterns themselves are seldom exactly filled. And it is this continuous cropping up of certain earmarks that differentiates one musical idiom from another.

A great deal of the subtlety of form in hot jazz improvisation is inexpressible in musical notation. In much of its detail it is as free and unpredictable as the emotions of the musicians who create it. But even at its freest, it is remarkable how often it exhibits characteristic, measurable elements.

All manifestations of hot rhythm are not precisely alike. As in most kinds of music, the limitations and aptitudes of the instruments upon which it is played, exercise an influence over the product of the jazz musician. Jazz ensembles are usually divided into three departments known technically as "brass," "reeds" and "rhythm." The first comprises the trumpets, trombones and other instruments of similar construction and technique. The second is represented by the clarinets, saxophones and such additions in the way of oboes, sarrusophones, flutes, and so on, as happen to be at hand. The third department is that of the drums and of instruments whose function in the ensemble is similar to theirs. The piano, the guitar, the banjo and the string bass are commonly included under this head.

Now this conventional division into three departments is not merely an arbitrary classification according to principles of instrument construction. It represents a differentiation of three totally distinct types of improvisatory technique. The hot intonations of a jazz trumpeter are quite different from those of a jazz saxophonist. The former's contribution to the ensemble is, as a rule, more oratorical, less precise and florid, than the latter's. And the jazz guitarist functions differently again from either of the others, hewing far more closely, even in his hot solos, to the strict line of fundamental rhythm.

The trumpet and the trombone are the declamatory, dramatic, emotional voices of the hot ensemble. More than any of the other instruments they approach the role of the human voice. Their inflections are usually closely related to the inflections of speech and song. They are the spokesmen of complete abandon, of ecstasy, of hysteria. Their utterances are the least formal, the least reserved and the most intimate. They speak like the voices of their manipulators, creating their own words in rhythm and tone-color. On the technical and physical side they are admirably equipped for this purpose. They have a larger practical range of dynamics than any of the other instruments. In the hands of a talented hot player they have an amazing variety of timbre, which is employed much as a vocalist employs the shades of color in his voice. The vibrations of trumpet tone are produced by a part of the player's own body. His lips function as do the vocal cords of the singer, and his medium is correspondingly flexible and responsive.

Hot trumpet (and to a slightly lesser extent trombone) solos thus tend to a greater rhythmic and dynamic freedom than do those of the other instruments. From the abstract musical point of view they are often chaotic, resembling recitative or even prose inflection. And the recitative and prose usually bear a close resemblance to Negro speech in their intonations. Crescendos and climbing phrases are infrequent. Explosive attacks are followed by dwindling tone and descending melodic curves. Artificial mutes, the device the Germans call *"flutter-zunge,"* and a dozen methods of lip and tongue manipulation result in a complete set of what we might with very little inaccuracy term vowel sounds. If the human voice formed an integral part of the generality of jazz ensembles, it might, as far as its musical function is concerned, be lumped with the trumpet and trombone as a member of the "brass."

Upon the "reeds" devolve the more lyric, what from the conventional point of view would be termed the more "musical," aspects of hot melody. While the "brass" produces the exclamations and the rhetoric, the melodic sense rests mostly with the "reeds." Their utterances are more integrated and civilized. Reed solos, as a rule, are more crystallized in musical form. Separate a brass solo from its context and it means very little. Separate a reed solo similarly and it will usually make some sort of musical sense. Hot reed improvisations tend to be more florid and complex than do brass. For these melodic peculiarities the instruments of the reed department have their appropriate aptitudes. The saxophone is among the easiest and technically most flexible of all wind instruments, and the clarinet is its close second in these respects. When the violin enters into the hot jazz ensemble, its functions are similar. All of these instruments are facile in the articulation of rapid legato passages. All are suited to a more florid, more precise and less emotional sort of expression. The subtleties of jazz "melody," as that word is commonly understood, rest principally with them.

Under "rhythm" are included those instruments whose principal function it is to maintain the constant throbbing that forms the foundation of the jazz edifice: what we have termed for technical purposes the "normal" or "fundamental" rhythm.

HOT RHYTHM

Their musical excursions are by no means limited, however, to a mere marking of the pulse in four-quarter time.

The "rhythm" instrument, par excellence, is the piano. I believe it was Stravinsky who remarked some years ago that the piano is essentially a percussion instrument. As employed by the jazz pianist it certainly falls into that category. It is, in fact, a percussion instrument of enormous resource. It possesses the drum's capacity to mark rhythm with incisive blows; and these blows can be struck with infinite gradations of loudness and softness, so that the subtlest contrasts in accentuation are possible. More than all this, the piano can support two or more rhythmic or melodic voices at once: a counterpoint of rhythms can be played on it with ease. Still more: it has a complete scale which permits no end of melodic and harmonic variation. It is little wonder that the piano occupies the chief place among all jazz instruments. Jazz without it is a rarity.

Much of the most detailed and complex rhythmic variation of the hot ensemble will be found in the piano part. Like the other instruments of the "rhythm" department, its role is a comparatively unemotional one. It lacks the personal intimacy of the trumpet, and the sustaining quality for lyric melody that the reeds possess. Its scale is fixed: the pianist cannot produce those alterations in intonation that are so important a part of the more vocal type of jazz melody. Its rhythms are for the most part rigid and precise. Among them the regular pulse of the fundamental rhythm usually has a dominating place.

Within far greater limitations as instruments, the banjo and guitar play similar roles to the piano's. Their common duty is to mark the pulses of the fundamental rhythm with a series of chords. In fulfilling this duty they are, like the string bass, merely a part of the rhythmic background. Occasionally, however, they step to the front and take on the task of full-fledged solo instruments. Though their tone, for this purpose, is comparatively weak, they can accomplish certain things which the piano and the remaining "rhythm" instruments can not. Their scale is not fixed like that of the piano. They can deviate, within the limits of their small sustaining power, from established intonation. And they can produce a certain powerful, twanging pulse for rhythmic purposes that is all their own. Like those of the piano, their rhythms are usually clearly defined.

The guitar has tended to replace the banjo in jazz ensembles with musical results that are not very different. The complexities of European guitar technique hold little place in the jazz guitarist's repertoire. As used by him it is, like the banjo, a "rhythm" instrument.

To the piano and banjo must be added those other indispensable members of the "rhythm" section, the drums. Among these instruments of indefinite intonation a variety of tone color will be found, ranging from the dull thud of the bass drum to the ticking sound produced by hitting the rim of the snare drum with a wooden stick. In the "sweet" ensembles a great deal of fancy percussion is usually added in this department, including wood blocks, Chinese tom-toms, gongs, cymbals, triangles, anvils, castanets, Chinese temple bells, vibraphones, xylophones, glockenspiel, celestas and similar exotic paraphernalia. Needless to say, such colorful resources do not lead to better or more interesting drumming. The drummer of the hot ensemble usually limits himself to a bass drum, a snare drum and a modest and easily handled assortment of kitchenware. It is the complexity and imagination of his drumming, rather than the instruments it is played on, that attracts musical attention.

The drummer's rhythms are incisive, absolutely precise, and indispensable to the accent and emphasis of a large ensemble. His role is usually a background affair, but its absence would be quickly noted. What the pianist often does as a counter-point of rhythms, a good drummer is able to do within a single rhythmic voice by differences in accent and tone-color. His role is even more mechanical and impersonal than that of the other "rhythm" players. From the musical point of view the tap dancer represents a branch of the jazz drummer's art. Though his footwork does not form a standard part of the jazz ensemble, its principles of rhythmic improvisation are precisely similar to those of jazz drumming. The differences, musically speaking, are only differences of instrumental medium. The feet of a Bill Robinson tapping on a wooden floor, and the drumsticks of a Gene Krupa tapping on taut calfskin are equivalent, and all the syncopative and polyrhythmic aspects of jazz rhythm are represented in both their arts.

It is hardly necessary to mention the role of the string bass here, or that of the bass tuba or sousaphone which took its place in earlier jazz ensembles. Both are background instruments, useful to mark elementary rhythms and bass notes of prevailing harmonies. Both are too unwieldy to offer much of interest to the present discussion.

Of the three departments of jazz orchestration the utterances of the "rhythm" and "reed" groups are the most easily notated. Indeed, where the "rhythm" instruments are concerned difficulties in the way of exact transcription seldom present themselves. As is to be expected, a larger proportion of mathematically precise rhythmic patterns is to be found in the solos of both "rhythm" and "reed" sections than in the more hectic, emotional playing of the "brasses." Among their contribution one finds polyrhythm and the other formulas of jazz theory embodied with considerable clarity. Yet even in the declamatory phrases of the "brass" there is often a surprising conformity, in rough outline, to the rhythmic patterns we have been describing. Hot rhythm is often more intense, more exciting, more complicated, faster, freer—above all it is more unpredictable—than sweet rhythm. But these are differences of quantity and quality. Where *type* of rhythm is concerned there is no difference. The same polyrhythmic and syncopative ingredients are basic to both.

The place of polyrhythm in hot jazz is a striking one. It is to be discerned in hot solos in all sorts of forms. Simple syncopation and the shifting of melodic elements from strong to weak beats also find no end of exploitation. Again, where polyrhythm is concerned, the preference is for the three-over-four superimposition, though superimposed cycles of other types are by no means infrequent.

Simple polyrhythmic patterns are to be found scattered through virtually all hot improvisation. Among countless examples the following taken from Benny Carter's (Chocolate Dandies) recording of the *Bugle Call Rag* (Columbia 2543-D) is typical: [1]

Here the superimposed triple rhythm of bars two and three

[1] In this, and the numerous subsequent examples notated from recordings, no attempt has been made to present the original key of the example. All examples are notated in C major for the sake of simplicity.

is defined by the two-note figure ♩ ♪ and the syncopation
has been prepared by the contrast of fundamental rhythm in
eighth notes which precedes it.

Benny Goodman, in the clarinet solo toward the beginning
of his recording *Who?* (Victor 25181-B), uses a number of
clear and extensively repeated polyrhythmic patterns, this time
defined by two eighth-notes and an eighth-rest:

Note again how the polyrhythmic cycles have been prepared
by measures and measures of clearly defined fundamental

rhythm, with strong beats intensified both by accent and by longer note values as in measures 9 and 10. When the poly-rhythm arrives in measures 13, 14, 17 and 18, it comes as a fresh contrast to the four-square rhythms that have pre-ceded it. Measure 19 contains another type of polyrhythmic figure, the cycles being represented by solid dotted notes (𝅘𝅥𝅮 𝅘𝅥𝅮 𝅘𝅥𝅮𝅘𝅥𝅮). This figure, common enough in hot jazz, is similar to the rhythm of the Charleston.

Such polyrhythmic figures as the foregoing are found in every sort of hot improvisation. Often, however, the cycles themselves are somewhat more complex in rhythmic structure. In Fletcher Henderson's recording of *Hop Off* (Brunswick 4119) the following saxophone solo exhibits a figure that is interesting both for its polyrhythmic use and for the prepara-tion it receives before it arrives in polyrhythmic form. The figure consists of five notes. The first of these is a high note; the next three are lower and describe a mordant-like orna-mentation (𝅘𝅥𝅮𝅘𝅥𝅮), and the last one is high again. In preparation the figure is successively stated as

and

HOT RHYTHM

Following a couple of bars interlude it returns in a series of polyrhythmic aberrations. The passage may be roughly transcribed as follows:

Other interesting polyrhythmic patterns are disclosed in the following trumpet solo from *Limehouse Blues* (Fletcher Henderson's recording, Decca 157-A):

Toward the close of Ellington's recording of *Harlemania* (Victor V-38045-A) the following peculiar polyrhythmic pattern appears:

HOT RHYTHM

Sometimes the crystallization of polyrhythmic patterns assumes very complex forms in which two or three cycles of different duration will be found simultaneously. A guitar passage in Louis Armstrong's recording of the *Savoy Blues* (Vocalion 3217) presents one of these curious superimpositions:

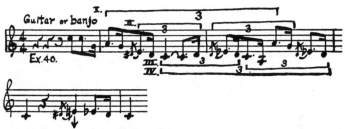

Here, using the recurrence of repeated melodic elements as a clue, four simultaneous cycles may be observed. Cycle I is defined by the salient note A which occurs again following the passage of three half-note values. Cycle II is defined by the melodic figure

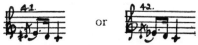

(The difference in notation between the two versions of this figure is negligible from the jazz point of view, as will be explained further on in the chapters devoted to scale.) The repetitions of this figure occur at intervals of three quarter-note values. Cycle III, also based on three quarter-note intervals, is defined by the important note C. Cycle IV, while it is perhaps only the sum of two cycles of three, is nevertheless distinct in that the C's defining it are both notes of long duration as opposed to the short C of measure 3 which acts in a defining capacity for cycle III. Such mathematically

93

perfect and complicated manifestations of polyrhythmic form are comparatively rare in hot jazz. But their occurrence bears striking testimony to the power of the polyrhythmic element in Negroid musical thought.

Another remarkable example of extended polyrhythmic cycles is to be found in Duke Ellington's recording of *Harlemania*. The initial trombone solo contains the following phrase:

Here the polyrhythmic cycles hinge on the little figure

From its first to its final appearance stretches a long cycle of three units (I), each of them comprising the value of two measures. From the same starting point a smaller cycle of one-and-a-half-measure (II) units brings in an intermediate appearance of the same figure. Cycle III represents merely the difference in time values between cycles I and II, and hence naturally forms another cycle of three units, this time of half-measure values. No one, confronted with evidence like this, can for a moment imagine that the polyrhythmic cycles of hot jazz are merely accidental combinations. The phenomenon is too regular in its appearance to be anything other than a fundamental characteristic of hot rhythm.

*   *   *   *   *

Two related and specialized uses of polyrhythm demand particular note because of their frequent appearance in hot jazz. These we might term for purposes of discussion the *jazz anacrusis* and the *cadential cycle*.

The first of these is a simple affair and easily described. An anacrusis, or what is known colloquially among musicians as an "up-beat," is that part of a musical phrase which precedes the initial bar line. Phrases that begin on the first beat of the bar (those of *God Save the King,* for example) do not have an anacrusis. A large number of musical phrases, however, commence on a weak beat preceding the first principal accent. In the phrase

"Auld Lang Syne"

for example, the initial C is an anacrusis. In European music the preference is generally in favor of the anacrusis which commences on the last quarter of the bar like the one quoted above. A search of any reasonably equipped musical memory will call to mind dozens of phrases beginning on this beat.

Now in hot jazz improvisation a very characteristic anacrusis is that which begins on the sixth eighth-note of the bar. Though this sort of anacrusis is rare in printed sheet-music jazz, examples of it in recorded jazz and Negro spirituals are constant. Listen to a jazz drummer as he enters at the close of a tap-dance routine and you will find

that he almost invariably commences three-eighths before the
entrance of the first main normal accent. The *tutti* that follows a hot solo, or a break, is very likely to make its entrance
on this same off-beat. The following example is chosen at
random from among the thousands to be found on hot recordings: *You Rascal You* (Mound City Blue Blowers, OKeh
41526).

The "cadential" cycle occurs commonly at the close, or
"cadence," of a phrase. The final note, occurring on the
first beat of the final bar, is preceded by a polyrhythmic
cycle of three, and the cycle is defined by a previous appearance of the final note itself. The recurrence of this phenomenon in all sorts of Negro music (hot and commercial
jazz melodies, spirituals, blues, and so on) is a very interesting thing. The following examples speak for themselves:

Lazy Bones (Mercer and
Carmichael)

Cadence from hot spiritual (Recorded
by E. P. Jennings) *Nora, Nora*

HOT RHYTHM

Sometimes arrived at by means of a hot rhythmic embellishment, it is common in jazz recordings:

Common distortion of
St. Louis Blues

Savoy Blues, Louis Armstrong
(Vocalion 3217) Close of
first trumpet solo

Cold in Hand Blues, Bessie Smith (Louis
Armstrong trumpet) (Columbia 140
64-D) Introduction

*   *   *   *   *

Irregular polyrhythmic patterns—those consisting of more than three units, and those which seem to show a tendency to expand or contract in the number of units of successive cycles —are not uncommon. They do not seem, however, to have anything like the fundamental place in hot rhythm occupied by the three-over-four superimposition. And their melodic manifestations are often imperfect from a mathematical point of view. Nevertheless, there are enough of them to warrant the conclusion that jazz musicians occasionally do think in other polyrhythmic terms than those of "secondary rag."

Reference has already been made to the type of poly-rhythmic pattern in which each cycle is represented by a single note. The commonest of these patterns seems to be the one in which two dotted eighths (quarters, sixteenths) pre-cede an undotted eighth (quarter, sixteenth):

etc. It is found in every variety of Negro music from the spirituals to jazz, and has often been misinterpreted by careless transcribers as a triplet.[2] Actually large triplets (♩ ♩ ♩) are uncommon in the musical expression of the Negro, although a great deal has been made of them in the arrangements of the sweet dance orchestras.

In hot jazz the single-note type of polyrhythmic cycle is very common. The last trumpet solo in the Mound City Blue Blowers' recording of *You Rascal You* (OKeh 41526) begins with a rhythm of this type, the polyrhythmic cycles occurring after the undotted value instead of before it:

Ex. 52.

The spiritual *Go Down Moses* as transcribed by Natalie Curtis-Burlin offers a somewhat more conventional example:

Ex. 53.

When Is-r'el was in E-gyp' Lan'.

[2] See p. 61.

98

HOT RHYTHM

Frequent examples of the Charleston rhythm, and the related polyrhythmic pseudo-triplet, are also found in the little-known, but remarkable, *Saint Helena Island Spirituals* [3] recently collected by Ballanta-Taylor. Indeed, the prevalence of polyrhythmic constructions in these spirituals intensifies one's suspicions of the accuracy of most other transcriptions of Negro religious music. Ballanta-Taylor's transcription of *Yo' Cyan' Find a New Hidin' Place*, for example, begins as follows:

Another spiritual in his collection begins:

Simple syncopation, particularly that of the anticipative variety, is, of course, a very common ingredient of hot rhythm. The slight anticipation of normal rhythmic stresses, such as appears in Louis Armstrong's initial trumpet solo in the *Mahogany Hall Stomp* (Vocalion 3055) has already been referred to, and requires no illustration.

The less obvious business of shifting melodic elements from

[3] Published by G. Schirmer, Inc., New York, 1925.

strong to weak beats, and the related matter of phrase distortion, offer some points of interest, however. Phrases like the following, from Louis Armstrong's recording of *Walkin' My Baby Back Home* (Vocalion 3217) present simple instances of this shifting process:

Trumpet (final solo)

In this case the shift is from weak to strong. The final E is the goal of the entire phrase. The first eight times the note E is attacked it enters on a weak beat. In bar 3 it makes its first appearance on a strong one: the third beat of the bar, and its final appearance is upon a still stronger beat: the first beat of the final bar. At first glance this sort of thing might appear to be accidental and unimportant from a musical standpoint. But a thorough comparison between jazz melody and European melody will show it, beyond a doubt, to be a fundamental characteristic of the former and a very infrequent associate of the latter.

Watch the behavior of the note E in the following saxophone passage from Duke Ellington's recording of the *Bugle Call Rag* (Columbia 2543-D); and try, if you can, to find its equivalent in European melody:

HOT RHYTHM

In no two successive appearances does this note occupy a
similar rhythmic position. Groups of notes are often similarly shifted. The beginning of the ensemble singing in the
spiritual *Who Was John?* as recorded by Mitchell's Christian
Singers (Melotone 6-07-58) shows the shifting of a two-note
pattern (F-A flat) from a strong to a weak beat:

A somewhat similar two-note shift, repeated in a very nearly
perfect cycle, appears at the end of a guitar solo (already
quoted) from Louis Armstrong's recording of *Savoy Blues*
(Vocalion 3217):

The distortion of repeated phrases is, of course, a very common device of the hot improviser. The process has already
been discussed in the preceding chapter. Its use in hot jazz
does not introduce any essentially new elements, and it hardly
requires illustration. These two examples show the use of a
simple phrase distortion in two different types of Negro music.
The little phrase itself, swinging between the tonic and the
flat or natural third of the scale, is so common in Afro-
American musical expression that it might almost be said to
constitute an idiomatic cliché.

JAZZ: HOT AND HYBRID

Spiritual *Tis Me, O Lord*
Curtis-Burlin Collection

Tis not ma sister but it's me, O Lord.

Wringin' & Twistin'. Trumbauer-
Beiderbecke-Lang
(Vocalion 3150)

Essentially this sort of distortion is merely a complex application of the process of shifting melodic elements from strong to weak beats and vice versa.

*   *   *   *   *

The syncopative shifting of melodic elements in hot jazz is not limited to those cases in which given tones, or even given groups of tones, are repeated with different accentual emphasis. There are cases in which a certain relationship between tones is the basis of the shift. A given type of melodic ornamentation, for example, may be similarly shifted with the effect of syncopation. The commonest device of this sort is that in which an appoggiatura, or passing note, resolves to a note of the prevailing harmony and is followed shortly by another similar ornamentation and resolution, the second ornamentation falling on a different beat of the bar. The effect is entirely dependent upon the harmonic substructure. A simple example will make the process clearer. In the following common jazz passage

102

all the notes except the G sharp and D sharp form part of the tonic harmony

The A added to the tonic C E G triad is frequent in jazz harmonization, and the resulting seventh-chord may be taken as a normal substitute for the plain tonic chord. Thus the passage contains two non-chordic notes; *i.e.* notes that are foreign to the main harmony of the measure. Each of them resolves, or passes on, to a chordic tone; and in each case the non-chordic tone and its resolution form a melodic pattern of distinct musical significance. Now, the first of these patterns (the G sharp followed by A) commences on a weak beat (the second eighth-note of the measure [4]). The second, however, (the D sharp followed by E) makes its appearance on a strong beat (the third quarter-note of the bar). The result is a syncopation, not of purely melodic elements, but of harmonic elements defined melodically.

This subtler type of syncopation will be found in all sorts of jazz. It does much to intensify the syncopation in the familiar motif of Confrey's *Kitten on the Keys:*

Ex. 63.

[4] Converted by "umpateedle" into a sixteenth-note.

In hot improvisation it is no less common than in more formulated jazz. In the third measure of the introduction to Benny Goodman's recording of *Who?* (Victor 25181-B) a very clear example presents itself:

The non-chordic tones (G sharp, B and G sharp respectively) and their resolutions define patterns which are repeated first on a strong beat (the third quarter of the bar) and then on a weak beat (the twelfth sixteenth, or twenty-fourth thirty-second, of the bar). A similar example occurs in the last trumpet solo of Ellington's *Bugle Call Rag* recording:

Another is to be found at the beginning of the clarinet solo in Henderson's recording of *Hop Off*:

In the preceding pages reference has been made, more than once, to rhythms found in Negro spirituals; and their simi-

larity to corresponding rhythms in hot jazz has been pointed
out. Certainly the large majority of the rhythms characteristic of jazz are likewise associated with a great deal of the
Negro's religious folk music. A preponderant number of the
spirituals transcribed in popular collections, on the other
hand, exhibit comparatively little trace of typically Negroid
rhythmic ingredients. This fact may be attributed to several
causes. There can be no doubt that the Negro is, on the
whole, somewhat more reticent rhythmically in his religious
expression than in the music of his secular celebrations. The
former expression, except in its more ecstatic moments, is
more likely to be constrained by the formalities of Christian
ritual. And music of slow and solemn attributes is less apt,
by its very nature, to bring forth the polyrhythmic efflorescences which grow so luxuriantly in the excitement of
faster and more exuberant tempos. Another cause of the apparent rhythmic conservatism of most published spirituals
may well lie in simplified and inexact transcription, sometimes
owing to the inexpertness of transcribers, sometimes to the
limitations of musical notation to which we have already referred. Still another cause may lie in the constraining results
of careful rehearsal in those cases where transcriptions have
been made from the singing of cultivated and artistically conscious Negro musicians. Probably all of these factors have
played some part where the rhythms of the "concert spiritual"
are concerned.

Yet certain characteristic elements may be observed even
in the structure of this rather formal variety of Negroid
music. Some of these have been referred to by quotation already. The common figure ♪ ♩. which led to the theory
of the "Scotch snap" as an ingredient of Negroid music is

one of these elements. The figure is, in fact, an incipient syncopation, and it is notable how frequently it appears in the sequence ♪ ♩. ♩. ♪ which has a polyrhythmic character about it, though it can hardly be classed as violently syncopative. Real, thoroughgoing polyrhythm does, moreover, appear here and there in the published collections, notably in Ballanta-Taylor's more primitive and unquestionably authentic *St. Helena Island Spirituals*[5] already frequently quoted.

The most satisfactory source for the student in this matter is, of course, the phonograph; and it is a tribute to the lack of imagination of our educational foundations that so little religious material of primitive Negroid character is available to the public in the form of recordings. The present writer has been fortunate in having access to a large private collection of phonographic material recorded by E. P. Jennings, a folklorist of North Bennington, Vermont. This collection has been recorded in an isolated district of central Alabama, and includes spirituals, sermons and related material taken under ideal conditions: that is to say during the actual circumstances of religious worship in primitive Negro churches. This material is far freer and far richer in characteristic elements than anything that appears in the published collections, and frequent reference will be made to it in the course of this discussion.

The commercial spiritual recordings made by Mitchell's Christian Singers have already been referred to for several examples. Two of these, *What More Can Jesus Do?* and *Who Was John?*, contain enough material relative to the present

[5] G. Schirmer, New York, 1925.

discussion to be worth more extended quotation. Both will
be considered further in their scalar and harmonic aspects.
At this point it is merely their rhythmic structure that is per-
tinent. Both consist, as do many fully crystallized spirituals,
of the repetition of a single stanza with various small elaborations in each repetition. The beginning of *What More Can
Jesus Do?* goes approximately as follows: (Only the principal
melodic voices have been outlined here.)

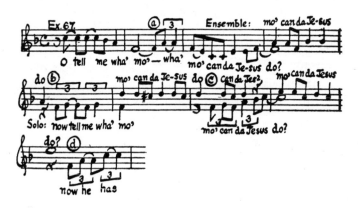

The characteristic anacrusis at a, the clearly defined polyrhythm of the solo part at b, c, and d, the phrase distortion
implied between b and c, and the use of anticipative syncopation in the solo passages, all stamp this quotation as unmistakably Negroid in the same sense that the term applies to
hot jazz.

Who Was John? is even more interesting from this standpoint: (Here again merely the principal voices have been
outlined.)

The shifting of the F-A♭ figure in the first and second bars has already been quoted. The prevalence of polyrhythmic superimpositions is worth noting, though most of them are of the ♪ ♩ ♩ ♪ non-syncopative variety. A remarkable example of shifting melodic elements is to be found in the behavior of the note F in measures 6, 7, and 8. On each successive appearance this note falls on a different rhythmic stress, even when the melodic pattern is to all other intents and purposes the same. Measures 6, 7 and 8 represent the statement and repetition of a melodic pattern of six notes, with a characteristic two-note answering phrase in the bass. Yet the rhythmic instinct of the Negro singer causes him to alter the pattern slightly at each repetition. And the alteration results in the shifting of the pattern's most salient note. In bar 6, F appears on the third quarter (strong) ; in bar 7 it appears on the fourth eighth (weak) ; in bar 8 it returns to the third quarter (strong). The shifting of this note from strong to weak beats and back again is in conformity with one of the most constant practices of the hot jazz musician.

Among the material recorded by E. P. Jennings several

fairly crystallized spirituals show similar rhythmic peculiarities. One of them, *Who Build Dis Ark? Nora, Nora* is polyrhythmic throughout, and concludes on a polyrhythmic cadential cycle which we have already quoted. Its form is simple, consisting of a solo, in which a short melodic figure is repeated over and over with slight variation, and an appended cadential figure which is repeated each time by the chorus. The resumption of this pattern, for a new stanza, usually begins with a characteristic polyrhythmic jazz anacrusis. A typical stanza follows:

At (a) and succeeding repetitions of the same figure a distortion of phrase occurs. Polyrhythm is constant in its manifestations, notable examples of it occurring at the cadences and just before the resumption of the new stanza in measure 10. From this and the preceding examples it is obvious that such rhythmic devices as polyrhythm, simple syncopation, phrase distortion, and the other rhythmic shiftings of melodic elements are to be found in the literature of the spiritual as well as that of jazz. Jazz may offer them in more complex and florid forms, but the basic principles themselves are very much at home in at least a portion of the Negro's religious music.

Chapter 7

THE GEOGRAPHY OF JAZZ RHYTHM

IN THE PREVIOUS CHAPTER we have attempted to describe in some detail the characteristic rhythmic patterns of hot jazz melody. A concluding glance at the material presented will show that all of these patterns depend for their effect upon a single rhythmic principle: the interruption of an established regular alternation of strong and weak rhythmic pulses. The interruption is accomplished by the shifting of recognizable repeated melodic elements from strong to weak positions and vice versa. The elements so shifted in repetition may be dynamic accents, notes, groups of notes, phrases, rhythmic patterns, patterns of melodic movement, particular types of harmonic ornamentation, even tone-colors. The shiftings may be apparent in distorted phrases, in what is known as simple anticipative or retardative syncopation, and in other sorts of melodic behavior. When the shifting occurs at regular intervals setting up repeated metrical cycles different from those of the established pulse, the result is polyrhythm.

Hot jazz rhythm may contain other peculiarities of an imponderable nature, peculiarities which cannot be expressed in musical notation or any similar form of measurement, and which arise from its improvised, extemporaneous character. But the patterns we have described constitute its measurable and technically discussible characteristics. And these characteristics have been found to be common to jazz and to much of the religious music known as "spirituals." These, then, are presumably the definable rhythmic characteristics of the Afro-American musical idiom.

How purely Negroid and how American are they? Several questions present themselves for solution. Are these the rhythms in which the African Negro casts the music of his primitive ceremonies? Are they found at all in the structure of the European art from which our conventional musical expression derives? Art they to be found in the music of the countries of Central and South America where large Negro populations exist? Are they found in any of the primitive musical idioms indigenous to the American continents—those of the Inca peoples of Peru, Ecuador and Bolivia, or of the North American Indian, for example? Is there any trace of them in the Anglo-Celtic religious, ballad and dance music brought to America by the white settlers, the music that still survives today in cowboy and hillbilly songs, in hymn tunes, and in the reels, jigs and hornpipes of New England and Southern "barn dancing"? When did these rhythms begin to appear as ingredients of the mass of American popular music?

Definite answers to all of these questions are not easy to find. But enough evidence can be gleaned from various sources to offer overwhelming support to the theory of Negro origin. It has been previously remarked in these pages that the systematic study of primitive African music is still in a very early stage of development. Musical ethnology as a whole is in its infancy. Africa remains a pretty dark continent even in more thoroughly exploited branches of ethnological research. The music of the African Negro is among the most primitive. It has no literature, no elaborate technical and theoretical system, no native aesthetic commentaries to offer the student seeking an understanding of its principles. It is not an "art music" in the sense that the musics of ancient Greece, Arabia, India, and China are. Its aesthetics are closely bound up with primitive religious ceremony, and hence are doubly difficult for the objective civilized mind to penetrate. From the purely technical standpoint of forms and methods, comparatively little data has been collected by European musicologists in Africa. Under the circumstances it is probably not an exaggeration to say that any sweeping generalization about the relation of African rhythms to jazz rhythms is, at present, unjustified.

Hints of an African genealogy are plentiful, however. Such trained observers as the late Natalie Curtis-Burlin, the late Henry Edward Krehbiel and the Negro musicologist Nicholas G. J. Ballanta-Taylor have noted certain similarities in structure between African and American Negro music. And more recently, evidence in the form of phonograph recordings has confirmed their observations. Jazz, as a general type of music, bears, of course, no relation whatever to primitive African tribal music. The question here is merely one of tracing certain isolated structural formulas, like polyrhythm, to African sources. But, so far, the facts available have been too meagre to support any very definite conclusions. Where our remaining questions are concerned, a little more definite light can be induced to shed itself.

Some of the rhythmic devices we have been considering are found sporadically, or in a limited application, in the music of Europe. The existence of syncopation in the music of the European masters is a commonplace that has been pointed out by almost every half-informed journalist who has written on the subject of ragtime or jazz. As a matter of fact it would be difficult to find a type of music from Borneo to Finland, or from ancient Egypt to the present, that did not make occasional use of syncopation in one form or another. It is one of the most elementary of rhythmic conceptions. Yes, jazz and Brahms quartets, in common with most music, are likely to exhibit syncopation. The significance of the point lies not in the existence of the syncopation but in the sort of syncopation used and the manner of its use. The syncopation in a Brahms quartet is likely to be a special effect, consciously used for its striking qualities; an incidental and occasional embellishment. In jazz, syncopation is a basic structural ingredient which permeates the entire musical idiom, and is to be found in virtually every measure of the music. In this respect the rhythm of jazz is far more closely related to the rhythms of Near Eastern and East Indian music than to those of European music. To the syncopation of the latter—a comparatively infrequent ornamental device—the syncopation of jazz has only a nominal resemblance. The function of syncopation in the structural scheme of the two arts is as different as could be imagined.

Where polyrhythm is concerned the muddlement of most writing on the subject increases. Both Don Knowlton and Aaron Copland find polyrhythm to be something unique to jazz and unprecedented in Western music, while the "syncopation" of ragtime is an overworked formula borrowed from the European masters. And their conclusions, quoted by such writers as the late Isaac Goldberg, have gained a certain currency. The whole point stands in need of clarification. As will be demonstrated in the next chapter, polyrhythm is not a characteristic of jazz as opposed to ragtime. The early rags were rich in polyrhythm at a time before the word "jazz" was ever heard of. In the second place there is no more reason to assume that the simple syncopation of early ragtime was borrowed from the European masters, than there is to assume that the polyrhythm of jazz is borrowed from the polyrhythm of the European masters. For polyrhythm is not only found in European music; it is a phenomenon of fairly common occurrence there, and has been used deliberately for its own specific effect by dozens of classical and romantic (not to mention modern) composers. The characteristic quality of jazz polyrhythm does not lie in the fact that it is polyrhythmic, but in the fact that jazz polyrhythm is peculiar in type and different in function from European polyrhythm.

The polyrhythmic superimposition of cycles of two over a fundamental rhythm of three units is very common in European music. It occurs, of course, only in compositions written in triple time. And since triple time is very infrequent in American Negro music and totally absent from jazz, this particular superimposition is not a characteristic of Afro-American rhythm.

The most familiar example of it is perhaps that which occurs in the *Minute Waltz* of Chopin:

Waltz in D Flat. Op. 64 No. 1

The famous "syncopated" chords in Beethoven's *Eroica* Symphony also belong properly to the two-over-three polyrhythmic category: [2]

[2] Other familiar examples of the two-over-three superimposition will be found in: Tchaikovsky's waltz *The Sleeping Beauty*; Schumann's piano concerto.

These are striking examples chosen at random from among many more. The two-over-three superimposition is also characteristic of a great deal of Spanish folk music.

When one leaves this two-over-three category one finds fewer examples in European music, though other types of polyrhythm are by no means unknown. Richard Strauss, in the introduction to his tone poem *Til Eulenspiegel,* allots to the French horn a polyrhythmic passage of arresting character. In this case there is a superimposition of cycles of seven over a fundamental rhythm of six—as peculiar a polyrhythmic pattern as one will find this side of Oriental music, and magical in its effect:

Again, however, this is a type of polyrhythm based on a fundamental rhythm of triple character ($\frac{6}{8}$) and hence foreign to the jazz idiom.

The three-over-four superimposition so characteristic of jazz is not common in the music of the masters. But it is to be found nevertheless. The following example from Mozart's remarkable *Quartet in F Major* (K 590, finale) is a perfect one:

Another striking example is to be found in the *Violin Concerto in E Major* of Johann Sebastian Bach. It has been quoted previously by Fox Strangways in his *Music of Hindostan* in connection with a study of Oriental polyrhythm:

Since the popularity of American ragtime and jazz has spread to the far corners of the earth, European modernist composers have been led now and then to imitate its rhythms in concert music. One of the earliest of these imitations is probably the *Golliwog's Cake Walk* from Debussy's *Petite Suite* which starts off with a polyrhythmic pattern reminiscent of early ragtime. Krenek, Stravinsky and others have followed in the same footsteps. Their efforts are, however, of no value to the present discussion, since they constitute pseudo-Negroid, rather than purely European music.

There can be no doubt, then, that certain forms of polyrhythm are found in European folk and concert music, and that even the three-over-four superimposition characteristic of jazz is not unknown in the works of the masters. But the commonest of the European superimpositions (that of two-over-three) is *never* found in jazz, and, for that matter, occupies only the position of an exceptional ornamental device even in the works of European composers. And the three-over-four jazz superimposition is, after all, a rarity in concert music. As in the case of simple syncopation, the European composer uses merely as an occasional embellishment a rhythmic device that forms a basic structural element in Afro-American music. The relation between the characteristic rhythms of jazz and those of European concert music is, then, so slight as to be negligible.

As to the appearance of Negro rhythms in the music of such tropical American countries as Cuba, Haiti and Brazil: that is a different story. The mixture of Negro and Latin idioms results in something different from jazz. But the characteristic Afro-American patterns are luxuriantly represented.

For more than a century Cuba has had an important share in the development of the world's popular music. The first form of Afro-American music to attract world-wide attention, in fact, came from there in early colonial times when the habañera, or *"contradanza criolla"* swept Spain and ended by becoming a characteristic form of Spanish folk music. In the process of naturalization by the musicians of the mother country, the colonial habañera undoubtedly lost a good deal of its Negro emphasis. But even in its Europeanized form it retained certain earmarks that are unmistakably Negroid. The transformation that it underwent by the time it reached Bizet's *Carmen* and Ravel's *Rapsodie Espagnole* curiously parallels the transformation of the tango, whose rhythms, apparently also originally Negroid, were similarly Latinized by the Argentines. Though the Spanish habañera and the Argentine tango differ greatly from each other today, internal structural evidence indicates that they are related, by origin, both to each other, and to such later Caribbean products as the rumba, the conga and the samba.

The historical authorities I have been able to consult seem divided on the origin of the tango. Some derive it directly from the habañera. Some give it a Mexican pedigree. As a modern form of popular music it, of course, owes its development and world-wide popularity to the Argentines. It is probably true that the characteristic rhythm of the habañera made an early entrance into the popular music of Mexico and many of the Spanish-American colonies. And even the theory of Mexican origin does not preclude an earlier Creole ancestry. The old Latin-American tune, *La Paloma,* is related both to the habañera and to the tango, and has served as a model for many a subsequent popular composer in Mexico and elsewhere. It was written by a Spaniard named Iradier who lived in Cuba in 1820. According to the Mexican musical historian Ruben M. Campos (*El Folklore y la Musica Mexicana*) [3] its rhythm was undoubtedly inspired by the "languid and cajoling" idioms of the Cuban dance.

In any case, habañera, tango and rumba all have a similar rhythmic structure. The traditional habañera, perhaps because it was brought into "civilized" musical circles at an earlier date, is the severest of the three. At first glance its characteristic bass figure

does not seem to offer any very striking Negroid qualities. But much that is lacking in the bare notes may have been explicit in the original Cuban emphasis with which this figure

[3] Publicaciones de la Secretaria de Educacion Publica, Mexico City.

was performed. The first three notes of the pattern are so placed as to outline a polyrhythmic grouping in cycles of three

and the repetition of the second note following a cycle lends further weight to this interpretation. Frequent use in habañera melody of "cake walk" figures (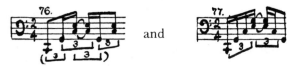 or

) is also a probable indication of polyrhythmic feeling. And the somewhat similar, and polyrhythmically more explicit, patterns that appear in the later tango, add another point in favor of the polyrhythmic theory.

When we get to the tango itself there is no question about the polyrhythmic character of these accompanying patterns. Such figures as

   and

are stock-in-trade, and melodic patterns like

are very common.

The rumba offers both the most obviously Negroid characteristics and the most authentic primitive musical structure.

THE GEOGRAPHY OF JAZZ RHYTHM

There is no doubt about its being Cuban. You can go to Cuba at any time and hear it. And you know, if you are careful to pick an unspoiled, spontaneous performance, that you are not dealing with something that has been written down, standardized and tampered with by the sophisticated musicians of three continents. Unfortunately the most interesting and authentic expressions of the Cuban rhythmic genius remain unrecorded for the commercial phonograph. But even in the available recordings by high-class and carefully rehearsed rumba orchestras there is enough of the primitive Negroid rhythm to illustrate our point. The incessant "basso-ostinato" of *Amor Sincero,* in Don Aspasiu's record (Victor 22483-B), consists of a continuous repetition (with occasional variation) of approximately the following pattern:

1. Wood-block (or similar native instrument); 2. Gourd rattles; 3. Guitar (merely outlined here)

The first half of this pattern is a counterpoint of polyrhythmic elements in which the guitar defines cycles of three both by accent and by melodic contour, and the native percussion instrument on the top line defines each cycle by a single stroke. The gourd rattles meanwhile preserve the fundamental rhythm. In the second half, the whole ensemble reverts to a simple definition of the fundamental rhythm. The total pattern is repeated over and over again, making a continuous alternation of polyrhythmic and non-polyrhythmic sections. This sort of accompaniment, comprising a continual swing back and forth between polyrhythm and simple rhythm, seems to be characteristic of a great deal of rumba music. A similar accompaniment of alternating figures will be found in the recording of the justly famous *Peanut Vendor* rumba which occupies the reverse side of the same disc:

Wood block
(or its equivalent)
Guitar
(merely outlined)

This recording also contains a hot trumpet part of some rhythmic interest.

That polyrhythmic structure is common in the music of Haiti, is attested by a number of notated examples of Haitian music collected by Harold Courlander in his book, *Haiti Singing*.[4] Several of these songs begin with the characteristic polyrhythmic anacrusis: [5]

A drum rhythm quoted by Courlander from the *Danse Canza*, runs as follows:

[4] The University of North Carolina Press, Chapel Hill, 1939.
[5] From the *Danse Rada*—a song of Guede Nimbo sometimes called Baron Samedi, Guardian of the Cemetery.

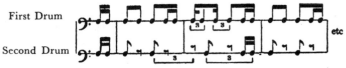

It is interesting to note that this example contains an alternation of polyrhythmic and simple rhythmic sections similar to that exhibited in the above-quoted rumba accompaniments.

Another collection of Haitian music, *The Voice of Haiti* [6] by Laura Bowman and LeRoy Antoine, contains a number of interesting polyrhythmic and other syncopated melodies. A *Bathing Song*, connected with voodoo ceremonies, begins with the following characteristic phrase:

An echo of the "Charleston" rhythm is found in a chant to the demigod Legba recorded in the *Voice of Haiti* collection:

The material I have quoted here on the music of the big Caribbean islands is necessarily somewhat sketchy. I have been unable to find any thorough published studies of the Creole music of such tropical American countries as Brazil,

[6] Clarence Williams Music Publishing Co., 145 West 45th St., New York.

Venezuela, Colombia and the smaller Antilles. Some day it is to be hoped, the various musical dialects of these regions will be thoroughly surveyed. Meanwhile a few additional clues keep coming in. If one is to judge Brazilian folk music by the artistic echoes of it that one finds in the compositions of Brazil's distinguished composer, Heitor Villa-Lobos, it is a type of music in which polyrhythm flourishes even more luxuriantly than it does in hot jazz. The samples of Brazilian music brought here by Carmen Miranda, Elsie Huston and the various samba orchestras of Hollywood and Broadway, confirm this impression. The Brazilian musical dialect may differ from the Cuban, but it is evidently a dialect of the same Negroid language. Another dialect, apparently, is to be found in the music of the "Calypso" singers of Trinidad whose improvised ballads, though somewhat severe and "Anglo-Saxon" in phraseological structure, are nevertheless chuck full of polyrhythm.

With what we know at present about the folk music of Latin America it is already possible to sketch a sort of musical geography of the Western Hemisphere south of the Rio Grande. Many of the details of this geography remain to be filled in. But the large outlines are growing increasingly clear. And it is obvious that, in the musical differences that separate its various areas, racial distinctions play considerable part. The northernmost musical area is the Mexican. Mexican folk music, on the whole, is characterized by a widespread use of Spanish rhythms and idioms, and a curious lack of elements attributable to the influence of Aztec, Mayan, or other pre-columbian peoples.[7] Just how the tradition of pre-columbian

[7] For further information of this curious fact see Otto Mayer-Serra's monumental *Panorama de la música Mexicana*, Mexico City, 1941.

music could have been lost among a people who are still at least 50 per cent pure Indian by blood, is a strange enigma. That the Aztecs and Mayas had their own music is proved by the existence of thousands of primitive musical instruments (many, apparently, with pentatonic scales) which have been unearthed from ancient tombs and dwellings. But what this music sounded like, nobody today has any idea. It may, of course, still exist in some isolated places not yet surveyed by musicologists. Rumor, and some wishful thinking on the part of Mexican writers, holds that it does. But records of it, either in print or on discs, are conspicuously lacking. The popular folk music that the Mexicans play and sing so fondly at their fiestas, bullfights and almost everywhere else under the hot Mexican sun, is conceived in a Spanish dialect that is without any significant trace of an Indian accent. In tunes on the model of *La Paloma,* the Cuban Negro influence is, of course, identifiable. But tunes of this type are so typical a part of the popular music of all Latin-American countries, that there is, at this date, nothing very distinctly Mexican about them.

Southward from Mexico, we come upon our next highly-developed folk music in the mountainous districts of Ecuador, Peru and Bolivia among the Quechua and Aymara Indians who constitute a large majority of the population of these three countries. The Quechuas, like the Mexican Indians, are not primitive tribesmen, but are the remnant of a once highly-civilized people. They are descended from the inhabitants of the old Inca Empire, and they have preserved both their language and their music more or less intact since pre-columbian times. The music, conceived in a musical language that is spread over practically the whole mountain area of these three countries, is still almost unknown to the outside world except for the musicological files of a few specialists. It is unquestionably the most highly developed indigenous music of the Western Hemisphere. It is not "primitive" in the sense that North American Indian music is. It is a true folk music. It bears almost no marks of European influence. It sounds more like Chinese or Scotch music than it does like Spanish, and it has a cool, almost prim charm that will never be forgotten by anyone who has heard it. The music of the Incas, unlike that of the Aztecs and Mayas, is still alive. Once the radio and the phonograph gain a foothold in the Andes, the Quechuas, like everybody else, will start imitating Frank Sinatra, and the only indigenous civilized music the Western Hemisphere possesses will be lost forever. It is shameful that our educational foundations, which have spent liberal sums to dig up Inca tombs and cities, have failed to finance any systematic plan to record this music. The tombs and cities will still be there a hundred years from now. The music is already beginning to disappear.

Now, the phenomenon of polyrhythm is totally absent from the music of the Andes, and, except for a few remnants in the anciently imported "La Paloma style," it is also totally absent from the popular music of Mexico. The former music is built with a curious irregularity of phrase structure [8] to which the polyrhythmic idiom is quite foreign. The latter (Mexican) is a distinctly Latin type of music, often appearing in three-four time, and containing none of the energetic syncopation characteristic of jazz or of Caribbean music. This Hispano-American style of music is not, as a matter of fact, limited to Mexico. It will be found all over Spanish-speaking South

[8] See Winthrop Sargeant: *Types of Quechua Melody*, Musical Quarterly, April, 1934, and Raoul and Marguerite d'Harcourt: *La Musique des Incas*, Edition Geuthner, Paris.

THE GEOGRAPHY OF JAZZ RHYTHM

America, flourishing with small local variations in the *pasillos* of coastal Ecuador, the *cuecas* of coastal Peru, in Chile, Argentina and wherever else popular composers of Spanish colonial traditions are active. One variant, with a very distinct flavor of its own, has become the dominant popular musical style of Argentina: the tango. As we have seen above, the tango shows evidences of a Caribbean origin. But as written and performed by generations of Argentines, it has taken on a proud, rather dignified emphasis that is quite foreign to the tropical abandon of Caribbean music.

All available evidence concerning the popular musical styles of Latin America points to one definite conclusion. Polyrhythm dominates the musical language only where Negroes form an important part of the population. This is the case in Brazil, Venezuela, the Guianas, Cuba, Haiti, Trinidad and the smaller Caribbean islands. It is also the case in the United States, where similar distinctions between Negroid and non-Negroid folk music exist. There are also purely white types of folk music in the United States. The cowboy songs of the Southwest, the Anglo-Celtic jigs, reels, hornpipes and sea chanties of New England, the type of commercial popular music known as "hillbilly," seldom contain any polyrhythmic constructions. There is no polyrhythm in *Home on the Range*, *Green Grow the Lilacs* or *Pistol Packin' Mama*. And, of course, there is none in the primitive music of the American Indian.[9] Polyrhythm is the distinguishing rhythmic mark of jazz, and every indication points to the fact that it is the contribution of the Negro, and of him alone.

[9] See monographs of Frances Densmore, Smithsonian Institute.

Chapter 8

THE EVOLUTION OF JAZZ RHYTHM
IN POPULAR MUSIC

JUST WHEN the Negro's rhythmic contribution began to appear as an ingredient of our popular music is something that would be very difficult to determine. The mass of sheet music turned out by the music publishing industry did not begin to show its effects in any overwhelming profusion until about 1900. The oldest New Orleans band of which present-day jazz players have any recollection (Buddy Bolden's) began flourishing at about the same date. On the other hand it is a certainty that American Negroid music was played and sung many years before it appeared in print. It is also a certainty that this music, in one variety or another, long preceded Bolden, not only in New Orleans but wherever else the Negro's influence was felt. Ragtime, introduced to New York by the white pianist Ben Harney in 1897, was a rural American phenomenon at least as early as the 'nineties. Its history undoubtedly went far back into the annals of "minstrelsy," and the minstrel show, a widely popular nineteenth-century form of American entertainment, dates, according to historians, from the early 'forties. Most minstrel troupes, of course, were white. But some were Negro. And the white ones, with their blackface tradition of burnt cork make-up, certainly reflected, in a more or less satirical manner, the Negro's characteristic habits as a musician and theatrical entertainer. It is not unlikely that the old Negro plantation entertainments after which "minstrelsy" was patterned, had their infusions of syncopated and polyrhythmic music long before even the minstrel appeared on the scene.

This, however, is a conjecture. The early nineteenth century did not have the blessing of the phonograph. Widespread recording of jazz and other forms of Negroid music did not appear until just before the first World War. Just how the music of the early minstrels and their Negro models sounded will never be known. It is a fact, however, that polyrhythm and other characteristic Negroid elements began to appear sporadically in printed sheet music several decades before the turn of the century. Their influence on the evolution of printed ragtime offers one of the most interesting features in the history of American popular music.

The earliest polyrhythmic outcroppings were somewhat reticent. But they are unmistakable. Even as far back as *Turkey in the Straw* or *Old Zip Coon,* which enjoyed popularity at least as early as 1834, we find evidence of the Negro idiom. The first half of the old melody is as prim and severe as any hornpipe. But the last half begins with the little figure

whose polyrhythmic character is pretty well defined. The rhythmic figure ♫♫ ♫ is not in itself necessarily Negroid or even necessarily polyrhythmic. It appears occasionally in old European dance tunes, and the mere presence of its note values here is not a completely convincing sign of Negro influence. What is far more important in this little phrase from *Turkey in the Straw* is the fact that the polyrhythmic structure is indicated by melodic contour as well as by note values. The initial E is followed by a second E exactly three sixteenths later, and the first G is followed by another G at a similar time interval. Thus the figure

is repeated as a polyrhythmic cycle; and in its repeated version its first note is moved from a strong beat to a weak beat. Here we have a peculiarity definitely and unmistakably Negroid.

Another old barn-dance tune with a polyrhythmic physiognomy is the *Arkansas Traveler*.

Here the polyrhythm is of an extended sort and the cycle is defined by a recurring figure of four sixteenth notes. The repetition is not precise where the notes themselves are concerned, the initial note of the sixteenth-note figure being changed from G to A. The other three notes, however, are exactly repeated, and the figure stands out sufficiently from the context—both in note values and by general contour—to qualify as a distinct and definite melodic feature. The units comprising the superimposed cycle of three are, of course, a measure in length. A small polyrhythmic relation will also be noted in the notes of the next-to-the-last bar, and in this particular version at least, the phrase closes on a polyrhythmic cadential cycle.

The "cake walk" figure (♪ ♩ ♪) which appears in the above mentioned phrase from *Turkey in the Straw,* has already been noted in connection with the habañera, the tango and the spirituals. As remarked above, the rhythm of the figure itself is not necessarily polyrhythmic. In Negroid music, however, it frequently appears with a melodic contour that leaves no doubt of polyrhythmic significance. And, in both its definitely polyrhythmic and its less definitely polyrhythmic forms, it is a favorite figure of the Afro-American.

This figure is perhaps the earliest polyrhythmic device to find consistent application in printed ragtime. It was a stock-in-trade formula among ragtime and country dance players in the 'nineties. Several old "buck and wing" dances in Harding's *Collection of Jigs, Reels and Dances* (copyright 1897) contain it. In the same collection will be found early precursors of the art of "jazzing the classics." In these early examples of musical mayhem the prime mutilator is the "cake walk" figure. Harding's version of *I Dreamt That I Dwelt in Marble Halls* from Balfe's *Bohemian Girl,* for instance, begins in this vein:

Ex 91.

etc.

It was the "cake walk" figure, too, that formed the principal basis of the art of playing ragtime as represented in Ben Harney's *Ragtime Instructor,* published in 1897. In this early treatise on the subject Harney also stressed the importance of beginning most of the measures in the right-hand part with a rest, an eighth rest in four-quarter, and a sixteenth rest in two-quarter time being considered appropriate. The following is an example of ragtime as written, and presumably as played, by Harney: (Requoted from Isaac Goldberg's *Tin Pan Alley.*)

Ex. 93.

It will be noted that these early essays in polyrhythm left the strong beats of the bar unmolested by syncopation. The "cake walk" figure is used in the old ragtime pieces either on the first or on the second beat of the two-quarter bar (*i.e.* 𝅘𝅥𝅯𝅘𝅥𝅯𝅘𝅥 𝅘𝅥𝅯𝅘𝅥 or 𝅘𝅥𝅯𝅘𝅥 𝅘𝅥𝅯𝅘𝅥𝅯𝅘𝅥). Its appearance on the second eighth (𝅘𝅥 𝅘𝅥𝅯𝅘𝅥𝅯𝅘𝅥 𝅘𝅥) or on the fourth eighth (𝅘𝅥𝅯𝅘𝅥 𝅘𝅥𝅯𝅘𝅥𝅯𝅘𝅥 𝅘𝅥𝅯𝅘𝅥) were apparently left for later innovators. The attendant slurring-over of the strong first and third eighths was evidently either too extreme a novelty for the nineteenth century rag composers, or too great a tax on their orthographic powers.

Even in the rags of the early nineteen hundreds a certain reluctance to override these beats with syncopations and poly-rhythmic cycles persisted. The prim, four-square structure of the old reels and hornpipes, put up a valiant defense against the new influence. But the development of polyrhythmic freedom was not to be denied indefinitely, even though the Anglo-Celtic tradition and the structural peculiarities of the European notational system were pitted against it. By the turn of the century the besieged strong beats began to yield here and there. The third eighth of the two-quarter bar (or the third quarter of the four-quarter bar) was the first to succumb. Tunes like Rose and Snyder's *Nothin' from Nothin' Leaves You*

became more and more common. "Two-steps" began to blossom forth with syncopations like

(*Trixie*—Erickson and Fassbinder)

The technique of rag piano arpeggios became enriched with such figures as

and by about 1904 a large number of tunes were making a special feature of this triumph over the now-helpless third eighth, as witness Bierman's *Pike Pikers:*

By 1905 not only third eighths but bar lines had been swept along in the current.

Full fledged polyrhythm defined by repeated cycles began to flourish more freely once the third eighth had been conquered. At first its appearances were tentative. The author of *Jagtime Johnson's Ragtime March* (1901) nearly succeeded in overriding the bar line with his polyrhythmic cycles in the following excerpt:

but he didn't carry it through. Nor did his cycles involve a true syncopation overriding the third eighth. It was not long, however, before the following polyrhythmic patterns became pretty well established:

Chicken Chowder—Giblin (1905)

Southern Melodies—Dubuclet (1905)

Chicken Charlie—Ballou (1905)

Polyrhythmic cycles passed beyond the bar line as early as
1905 in Larry Buck's *Freckles Rag*:

Ex.100.

From the same year dates the earliest extended example of
polyrhythm in absolutely perfect repeated three-note cycles
that the present writer has come across. Seventeen years later
Zez Confrey was exploiting the principle in *Kitten on the Keys*
and similar pianistic ventures. In 1905 Jos. Northrup and
Thomas R. Confare in their *Cannon Ball, A Characteristic
Two Step*, wrote as follows:

Ex 101

They were, no doubt, merely writing down what had been a
stock trick of ragtime pianists for some time. But the appearance of the formula in black and white was at least a rarity at
the time *Cannon Ball* was written. In the years immediately
following, however, it became one of the most characteristic
devices of the sheet-music rag.

The years that followed—from 1905 to 1910—might, in
fact, be spoken of as comprising the "golden age" of ragtime. It was during this period that it reached its heyday as

a national institution. America was beginning to dance as never before in its history. Formerly a great deal of our popular music had been written to sing. Now there was an unappeasable need for music to dance to. The sentimental song was giving way, in the public favor, to the "two-step" and its various Negroid derivations. And Tin Pan Alley was scouring the country for material to fill the new requirements.

A purely vocal type of music could never have filled them. The song, as a medium, was too limited in rhythmic possibilities. Ragtime was essentially an instrumental art. Few of the best rags offered melodies that could be sung. None of the really good ones had vocal refrains or were encumbered with words. The song writers attempted for years to capitalize on the trend by writing vocal tunes in which texts extolling the virtues of the dance were accompanied by slightly "ragged" piano accompaniments. The results were usually feeble imitations. One need only examine the so-called ragtime songs of such writers as Irving Berlin and George M. Cohan to be struck with their unimaginativeness in comparison with the real rags of the period. The rags were written by instrumentalists who knew their instruments intimately and exploited their practical potentialities. Few of the big commercial names of Tin Pan Alley knew enough about music in the practical sense to turn out acceptable rags.

The dominating instrument of the period was the piano, and the good rag composers were usually pianists. The standardized dance orchestra had not yet appeared on the scene. The saxophone did not make its entry as a standard component of the jazz ensemble until about 1916. The jazz arranger, whose function in turning vocal "tunes" into acceptable dance music was so important to Tin Pan Alley's later activity, was as yet an unknown quantity. The phonograph had not yet made orchestral dance recordings available to every hamlet and isolated farm-house in the country. The piano, plus or minus a few additional instruments, was what the generality of Americans danced to. Equipped with a "player" mechanism and perforated rolls it took the place later occupied by phonographically recorded music. It was to be heard in every small "nickelodeon" where the products of the budding movie industry were displayed. A player piano was the pride of every reasonably prosperous rural family. And the ability to play some sort of elementary ragtime on the mechanically unassisted instrument was daughter's most admired "accomplishment."

It was under these social and mechanical circumstances that the rag reached its nation-wide popularity. The Negro's piano technique—a curious combination of digital expediency and native rhythmic sense, operating upon a highly complex civilized musical instrument—had already developed into a characteristic idiom. The dance craze and the universal accessibility of the piano combined to make it, for a time, the popular idiom of the whole country.

As it existed between 1905 and 1910 the rag offered the most intricate and interesting rhythmic development that has ever been recorded in our popular printed sheet-music. The rag writers of the early nineteen hundreds used every formula of syncopation, phrase distortion, and cyclical rhythmic structure that ingenuity could contrive. Polyrhythm flowered exuberantly. By 1909 every aspect of the three-over-four variety had been exploited, including complex superimpositions and exact repetitions of cyclical phrases. None of the sheet music industry's subsequent efforts have shown anything of comparable technical complexity. Revivals, in the nature of trick piano compositions, did appear from time to time. Some were clever. Confrey's famous polyrhythmic pieces were essentially rags, and Confrey used the old rag formulas with considerable adroitness. But he added little that will not be found in the rags of the century's first decade. Almost every rhythmic formula subsequently fashionable in "sweet" jazz made its first printed appearance prior to 1910.

The rags of the "golden age" added a freer use of over-lapping rhythmic devices to the simple syncopated formulas that had been prevalent up to 1905. The "cake walk" figure, though still persisting here and there, died out as a funda-mental ingredient around 1910. By 1915 it had become vir-tually extinct in popular music, except as a special archaic effect. An even earlier death was accorded that nauseating little figure that used to interlard the vocal phrases in so many of the early rag accompaniments

Ex. 101½

and that never ceased to remind one of a fourth-rate brass band playing a badly arranged march.

The overriding of the third beat continued in such stock right-hand figures as these:

Small phrase distortions and displacements

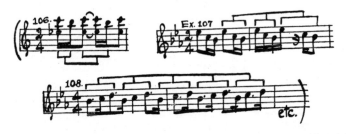

were a very prevalent source of variation. The cadential figure

in use at least as early as 1905, enjoyed continued popularity, and is still to be found in the jazz artist's bag of formulas.

These, however, were among the commonest everyday recipes, and were used in nearly every rag of the period. The more imaginative rag composers occasionally turned out more striking tricks of rhythmic structure. Polyrhythm defined by melodic contour (always a more subtle and less mechanical device than polyrhythm defined by exact repetition) got a fairly early start. Northrup and Confare's *Cannon Ball*, of which mention has already been made, contained many passages like the following

in which cycles formed by the movement of the melody were repeated at different pitches. About 1909 it became fashionable to intensify the polyrhythmic form of a melody by adding extra notes or chords at certain points in the cycles:

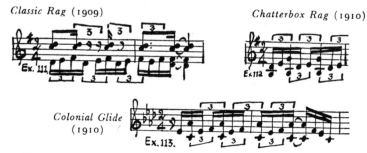

Classic Rag (1909)

Chatterbox Rag (1910)

Colonial Glide (1910)

The author of the *Texas Steer Rag,* George Botsford, defined polyrhythmic cycles by melodic contour with a characteristic use of both hands which attained some popularity:

The same composition, a rather remarkable rag by the way, contained some interesting superimpositions of simultaneous cycles:

Earl K. Smith's *Hot Ashes* published in the same year (1909) possessed the following peculiar example of the same phenomenon:

By 1910 the rag had become enormously popular, and decadence set in. Public demand brought about wholesale production, and by this time even the least gifted of Tin Pan Alley's hacks knew the tricks of the trade. The rags of subsequent years were numerous and mostly of poor quality. Old formulas were done to death, and individual ingenuity disappeared from the art of rag composition. Contrary to popular belief, and to his own published statement,[1] Irving Berlin was far from being the instigator of the ragtime craze. By the time the uncharacteristic and rather unimaginative phrases of *Alexander's Ragtime Band* appeared in print (1911) the rag, from a creative point of view, was already well on the decline.

The ballyhoo of the song publishing industry, of course, would have it otherwise, and even such supposedly dispassionate chroniclers as the late Isaac Goldberg have been taken in

[1] *Words and Music.* By Irving Berlin. Green Book Magazine, July 1915, p. 104 (See Goldberg, *Tin Pan Alley*, p. 239). The popular and wholly erroneous belief that Irving Berlin had something to do with the "invention" of ragtime has been further intensified by a recent motion-picture called *Alexander's Ragtime Band.*

by its misstatements. If one goes direct to the published popular music of the period for one's information, one is immediately struck by the fact that Tin Pan Alley's contribution was, here as elsewhere, largely a matter of commercial exploitation. The best rags were not written by the one-finger pianists and astute business men whose names dominated the industry. In fact few of the best rags even issued from New York. On the covers of the earliest and most imaginative of them the names of such publishing houses as Victor Kremer, McKinley and W. C. Polla of Chicago, Herzer and Brown of San Francisco, Howard and Browne of St. Louis, and Darrow and Sharp of Denver, appear quite as often, or oftener, than those of the New York publishers. In the "golden age," the rag was literally a national type of musical expression. Good rags were written all over the country. Exploitation by Tin Pan Alley came later, and with it came a cheapening of the product.

The transition from ragtime to jazz has also been made the subject of a great deal of misinformed and unsubstantiated writing. Styles in our popular music have, of course, changed gradually. "Sweet" commercial jazz today is different in many respects from the ragtime of 1910. It is orchestral where ragtime was pianistic. It is suave and sophisticated where ragtime was jerky and boisterous. Its melodies are vocal, based on tunes that are originally created as songs. Its composers, and what is more important, its arrangers, are likely to be eclectic in their choice of musical material. Its harmonic and orchestral effects are often borrowed from the romantic and impressionistic composers of Europe. Its general character is more romantic and sentimental, less primitive, than that of ragtime. It is also a more complex product, in which the work of the composer appears as a mere scaffold for the more important activities of the arranger and the instrumentalist.

Despite these and other differences, however, it is difficult to lay hands on a rhythmic formula in commercial jazz that was not represented earlier in ragtime. One often hears the theory advanced that polyrhythm is a characteristic of the former and was absent in the latter. Both Don Knowlton and Copland subscribed to it. But the facts do not support it. Polyrhythm, even in its most explicit forms, was, as we have shown, an outstanding characteristic of ragtime, and appeared in exactly repeated cycles at least as early as 1905, which was long before commercial jazz, as such, was even heard of.

This is not to say that commercial jazz derives wholly from the printed rags of 1910, or that a "sweet" jazz piece is merely an orchestrated rag. Jazz draws much from the vocal aspects of Negro music, and these aspects were necessarily absent from such a purely instrumental expression as the rag. The blues, publicized and brought to national popularity by W. C. Handy just as the rag craze was beginning to die out, undoubtedly made a powerful contribution to the technique of the commercial jazz artist. Part of this contribution led to greater harmonic and melodic subtlety. Ragtime had been rich in the percussive rhythmic elements of the Negro idiom. But it had contained little trace of the Negro's miraculous instinct for harmonization, and no trace whatever of his beautiful and characteristic style in sustained vocal declamation. These things, or their pale reflections, entered the commercial jazz artist's tool kit with the advent of the blues; and the wind instruments of the jazz band provided him with a pliable medium for their exploitation. We shall have occasion to refer to this development more fully in the chapters on scale and harmony.

Influenced by the blues, the temper of popular music as a whole became warmer, its melodies smoother and its tempos somewhat more deliberate. The enormous popularity of the tango in the early 1910's testified to the need for a more sustained, romantic type of music to relieve the incessant clatter of the rag. But the tango, with its distinctly Latin emphasis, remained an exotic importation. The blues offered an even slower tempo and a more singable melodic line than the comparatively hectic tangos of the period, and coupled these qualities with an idiom that was already deeply established in the American musical consciousness. They also offered Tin Pan Alley an opportunity to get the public appetite focused on "tunes" again, which must have been somewhat of a relief to Tin Pan Alley's "composers" after a harassing decade of ten-finger pianism.

The blues contributed to the development of the characteristic "sweet" jazz style that consists of a sustained melody moving over a slowly throbbing accompaniment. The division of the standard jazz ensemble into brasses and reeds on one hand and "rhythm" instruments on the other was probably a result of the blues type of structure. The vocal lament became the province of the wind instruments, while the continuous Negroid rhythmic undercurrent fell to the piano, banjo, guitar, drums and other instruments of percussive quality.

The "break," another distinct jazz characteristic, also entered the general field of popular music with the blues influence. This cadenza-like device will have to await discussion in another connection. It provided a new vehicle for variation and, since a great deal of jazz variation is rhythmic, it deserves passing mention here. Its principal significance, however, was as a development in musical form. It involved no new rhythmic principle.

The style of American commercial dance music, then, changed considerably between 1910 and 1920 when what was popularly known as ragtime passed over into what is popularly known as jazz. But this change in commercial popular music —important as it was in the fields of melodic style, harmonization, instrumentation and musical form—was not primarily a change in rhythmic structure. The blues, a type of jazz that had existed in improvised form at least since the 1890's, acted as a sort of catalytic agent. It provided Tin Pan Alley with new ways of dressing up the Afro-American rhythmic ingredients that had flowered in ragtime. But the basic ingredients themselves did not change.

The history of ragtime, or more precisely of the piano rag as it existed between 1900 and 1910, is that of a special autonomous branch of jazz. For musical scholars it offers a convenient, well-documented literature relating to what was at the time the most widely popular form of popular music. It was not, of course, the only type of jazz that was being created between 1900 and 1910. The New Orleans jazz tradition of improvisation, a form which bore very little relation to it, was flourishing at the same time. Later, with the ascendancy of "hot" jazz in the 1920 and 30s, the New Orleans style was to have a marked effect on popular music as a whole. But at this period it was a regional development, almost unknown to the nation-wide public. Commercial "sweet" jazz reached the public at about the time of the first World War when it succeeded ragtime and the first big national vogue of the tango. With it came the entrance of the word "jazz" into the national vocabulary, and the awareness of jazz as a definite and different type of music.

But these happenings were basically a matter of mores rather than of music. In their restless search for novelty, the music publishers and the popular dance band leaders reached into the flowing stream of Afro-American music and came up with a trick or two that could be exploited as the popular musical rage of the moment. The changes they thus brought about were changes of fashion rather than changes in the basic character of the jazz idiom. The history of these changes is a fascinating subject. But the evidence given here shows that jazz as a distinct type of music existed long before America discovered it. Where rhythm in particular is concerned, the Negro idiom was present even before what is popularly known as the "ragtime era" got started.

Chapter 9

THE SCALAR STRUCTURE OF JAZZ

WHERE THE SCALES of jazz are concerned the problem of defining the Negro contribution becomes more complicated. In its rhythmic aspects hot jazz melody may be purely Negroid. But in its scalar aspects it is very much influenced by European factors. Harmony, as the jazz musician employs it, is a purely European structural principle. The Negro may, and does, show a preference for certain harmonic constructions, and this preference may lend his harmonization a special character, somewhat different from that of European harmonization. But the harmonies he uses are European harmonies none the less.[1]

Now, when harmony enters into the musical scheme, melody tends to conform to its dictates. Most melodies in Western music grow out of implied or expressed harmonic substructures. In adopting European harmony the Negro has also adopted its tendency to govern his melody. Jazz melody is thus no simple combination of well-defined Negro and well-defined white ingredients, but a complex fusion of psychologic as well as abstract musical elements and influences. Jazz harmony, in

[1] African natives do use certain chord-like structures in their singing, as do also the most primitive "shoutin'" congregations of the South. But the principle of harmonic *progression* common to all Western music (including the spirituals and jazz) seems to be a peculiarly European development.

the first place, offers a Negroid selection of European materials. Jazz melody—much of it at least—offers a Negroid selection of scalar materials growing out of this Negroid selection of European harmonic materials. The nature of the resultant product is so involved that it is hard to say what is characteristically Negroid and what is borrowed.

However, there undoubtedly exist in jazz certain scalar features that are original with the Negro. There is no doubt, for example, of the striking individuality of blues melody; of the fondness of the spiritual singers for the flatted seventh of the scale; of the prevalence of pentatonic scales in the spirituals; of the characteristic quality of the curious deviations in intonation practiced by the hot jazz musician.

Abbe Niles, in his introduction to W. C. Handy's *The Blues: An Anthology,*[2] has remarked upon the tendency of the blues singer (or player) not only to employ the flatted third and seventh in the major scale, but to "worry" those tones when they occupy an important place in the melody, slurring or wavering between flat and natural. The practice, which is definitely a characteristic of Negro musical utterance, is by no means limited to blues and hot jazz intonation, but is found in the spirituals, where it must have proved a stumbling block and a source of inaccuracy to more than one of the transcribers of our popular spiritual collections. It is also found in the intonations of Negro speech when the speaker is under the stress of intense emotion, and it is unquestionably one of the oldest earmarks of Negro musical expression, antedating by far the official appearance of the blues and the incorporation of blues harmony and melody into the popular Tin Pan Alley idiom.

[2] Albert and Charles Boni, New York, 1926.

148

THE SCALAR STRUCTURE OF JAZZ

This peculiar deviation from European usage, the pentatonic propensity, and other similar matters invite classification under the conventional heading of "scale." Blues intonation is undoubtedly Negroid; pentatonicism may possibly be borrowed, but it is so frequently found as to constitute an Afro-American musical characteristic; other scalar constructions, borrowed or not, may be identified with the idiom through their frequent appearance in Negroid music. And even where borrowing has taken place there is a Negroid element in the peculiarities of taste that have caused the Negro to select certain ingredients of the European system and to reject others.

The business of comparing scales as between one type of music and another, however, is one that leads easily to misconceptions. A "scale" is presumably the aggregate of relative pitches used in a given form of music. It is possible to specify that the major and minor diatonic scales with certain chromatic alterations have been the basis of most classical European music; that the Greeks and mediaeval Gregorians used seven-tone modes of various kinds; that Scotch folk music and the melodies of the Chinese are predominantly pentatonic; that the Hindus use a profusion of five, six and seven-tone scales based on a theoretical subdivision of the octave into twenty-two *srutis,* and so on. But such comparisons are facile and tend to oversimplify a very complex relationship. A Western melody, built as the superstructure of a harmonic accompaniment, is very different from a Hindu *raga* which does not imply any such accompaniment. The actual notes involved may bear a similar relationship to each other in pitch, but the principles of their application are totally different. A piece of Gregorian monody, based on a system of modes, is melodically in a different dimension from a pentatonic Chinese song based on a

149

system of twelve *lis*. To compare the scales involved is a little like comparing the vocabulary of a sonnet with the vocabulary of a cross-word puzzle. Both consist of similar elements. But the functions to which these elements are put differ radically.

This problem presents itself when the scalar constructions of the American Negro's music are compared with those of European music. Presumably an African construction has been imposed, or an African influence has been brought to bear, on a European scalar system. The native African has no harmony in the European sense of the word. Are the intonations of Negro music to be considered as independent, in their relationships, of the harmonic system on which they have been grafted? Sometimes it seems possible to consider them in this light and to speak of such a thing as an Afro-American scale. Elsewhere the derivation from harmonic sources is so obvious that one is constrained to consider the melody as a variety of, or aberration from, Western melodic usage—that is, as governed by a harmonically-dominated "scale" in the Western sense of the term. An examination of the material presented in this and the following chapters will show that this is not mere academic hair-splitting. Much of the primitive American Negro's musical, or quasi-musical, expression is independent of any definitely formed contrapuntal background. And yet its scalar relationships are quite well defined.

More important, perhaps, than the discussion of scale as a cut-and-dried mathematical relationship of relative pitches, is the discussion of the melodic behavior of the individual tones. Are certain tones used more often or held longer than others? Are certain tones likely to be followed or preceded by certain other tones, forming characteristic melodic patterns? Are some tones used incidentally and passed over quickly as mere embellishments? The characteristics of melodic movement are often more vital in defining musical style than are the abstract relationships between pitches. Four pentatonic melodies, one by a Chinese, one by a Negro, one by a Scotchman and one by a Peruvian Inca Indian, may be quite similar in the relative pitches of their tones, but the patterns in which the tones follow each other may differ greatly.

With some reservations in mind, then, let us consider the abstract scales common in jazz and in other types of Afro-American music. The first to present itself, since it has been so much talked about in connection with the Negro, is the pentatonic—that particular pentatonic scale designated by Helmholtz [3] as No. 4. It consists of a root, major second, major third, perfect fifth and major sixth

and its general character is major.

This scale is found in hot jazz and in hot spirituals, though it is by no means the most characteristic scale of either. In the conventional published spirituals it is very common. A survey of Nathaniel Dett's edition of *The Hampton Institute Spirituals,* which may be taken as representative, shows that spirituals with pentatonic melodies constitute about one-third of the total. The next commonest scale exhibited in these spirituals is the hexatonic formed by adding a perfect fourth to the above-mentioned pentatonic.

[3] *Sensations of Tone,* p. 259.

These two scales, taken together, account for something more than half the melodies in the collection. Notable is the scarcity of the minor scale and of other pentatonic scales than the one we are considering. With or without the added fourth this pentatonic series, then, seems to constitute a very dominating scale of the spirituals as they have been transcribed for concert use.

The same scale is very popular in sweet jazz. A large percentage of the Tin Pan Alley tunes from which sweet jazz derives is written in it. Here, however, it can scarcely be attributed to a Negro origin, since pentatonicism has always been an outstanding characteristic of Anglo-Celtic religious and secular song, and was common in American sentimental ballads, rural dance music and hymn tunes long before the Negro's influence was felt in any of these fields.

It is, in fact, difficult to make the pentatonic scale a basis of differentiation between Negroid and other music. The scale itself is perhaps the most universal of all scales. It is indigenous to every continent. Many civilized musical cultures and many folk idioms have employed it independently of each other. The American Negro's use of it, moreover, is very similar to the white's. A spiritual like *Deep River* contains phrases that might be Scotch as far as scale and melodic movement are concerned.

But it is just as difficult to prove that the pentatonic was borrowed outright from the European idiom. The scale exists among the native Africans. Indeed, judging from the meagre fund of African material that has come to this writer's attention, it holds a very important place in African music. The most likely explanation is that the Negro found in the pentatonic of the Anglo-Celtic idiom an element which struck a sympathetic chord in his own racial memory, and which adapted itself perfectly to the methods of harmonization which he was learning to employ in his American environment. The European harmonic influence has undoubtedly been an important one, and has contributed a great deal to the formation of the melodies of both the spirituals and jazz. The prevalence of the pentatonic scale in the spirituals may possibly be attributed to the fact that it formed the most obvious common denominator between the native African idioms and the harmonically dominated music of the white hymn tunes.

Another scale which has been associated with the Negro in this country is the harmonic minor with or without an optional alteration of the fourth degree forming a so-called "gypsy" scale:

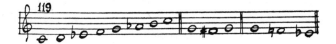

It has been made the basis of many pseudo-Negroid Tin Pan Alley tunes (*You Rascal You, St. James Infirmary Blues,* etc.) and is found in simpler forms (usually with missing 6th degree and unaltered or missing 4th degree) in the published spirituals (see *See Fo' an' Twenty Elders, Go Down Moses*: Hampton Collection, etc.).

Its appearance is a phenomenon somewhat difficult to account for. Its minor modality is not to be confused with the characteristic modality of the blues, with which it has nothing in common. Its third degree is minor, but its seventh degree is major, often with a definite "leading tone" tendency toward the tonic above—an unusual feature in Negro melody. In many cases the melodies based on it are so obviously mere embellishments of common European folk harmonies as to appear spurious—or at any rate not characteristically Negroid. This is true, for example, of both *You Rascal You* and the *St. James Infirmary Blues*, either of which might easily be a Russian Jewish or Balkan folk song as far as melodic physiognomy is concerned. On the other hand, the spiritual *Go Down Moses* seems to possess a certain flavor of authenticity.

Minor spirituals of the *Go Down Moses* variety are, however, extremely rare.[4] Only about five per cent of the spirituals in the Hampton Collection are minor in modality, and when one had taken out the obviously derivative ones the percentage is still lower. In other fields of Negro music the rarity of the minor mode is still more striking. In jazz as a whole the minor melody is exceptional; and in hot improvisation it will only be found, I think, where the player is attempting to stick to a published tune of minor modality. It is probably true that more than one white or conventionally educated Negro musician has written imitation Negro folk melodies in this scale, mistaking it for the more subtle and characteristic scale of the blues. In the singing and playing of the more primitive American Negro, however, it is rarely heard.

The harmonic minor with raised fourth degree is, of course, common among the Semitic peoples of North Africa and Asia Minor, and it is not altogether impossible that the Negro may have brought with him to America the musical fruit of an earlier contact with these peoples. Krehbiel[5] has hinted at

---

[4] In his book, *Afro-American Folksongs* (G. Schirmer, 1914) the late Henry Edward Krehbiel gives the results of a modal analysis of 527 Negro songs and spirituals. The number of minor songs in the total was only 62, as against 331 major, 111 pentatonic, and 23 songs with mixed or vague scales. Of the 62 minor melodies only 19 had a leading-tone. None had the raised fourth of the "gypsy" scale.

[5] *Afro-American Folksongs*, p. 91.

such a possibility. The question is a speculative one, however. In the cases where a European harmonic basis is obvious there is little possibility of African influence. In those rare spirituals like *Go Down, Moses,* proof would be hard to establish. The minor mode is, at any rate, scarcely an outstanding characteristic of Afro-American music.

The common major scale of Western music has, in fact, far more widespread currency both in sweet jazz and in the published spirituals than has the minor. The pentatonic and the hexatonic scale, consisting of the pentatonic with an added fourth degree, have already been referred to as the commonest scales of the published spirituals. The transition from this hexatonic

to the common major scale involves merely the addition of a single tone. In view of the close contact of the Southern Negro with white secular and religious music of major modality it is little wonder that the seventh degree should have crept over into Negroid music, especially since it formed an important chordic component in the harmony that the Negro absorbed from the whites.

It is notable in this connection, however, that even where the seventh degree of the major scale appears in the spirituals and in jazz, it seldom functions as the "leading tone" of European melody. The Negro's melodies commonly approach their final notes from above by way of the second (or in the blues by way of the lowered third) degree, or from below by way of the sixth degree. These pentatonic and other tendencies are apt to remain even though the seventh degree appears freely as an embellishment and as a component of the accompanying harmony. Further discussion will be given these cadential matters in the chapter on "Harmony."

*   *   *   *   *

Though all the scales mentioned above are found here and there in hot jazz, the most characteristic scale of this type of music is another, and more definitely Negroid one. Its appearance, however, is not continuous, and is dependent on certain melodic and harmonic circumstances which must be described before proceeding further. Hot jazz melody is improvisatory, but its structure is held to a coherent formal pattern which restrains it from complete chaos. This coherent pattern is provided by the harmonic sequences of the underlying accompaniment. The harmonic structure of most hot jazz is very simple, and is borrowed in its principles of sequence from European models. The selection of European models has, of course, its Negroid aspects. The Negro musician shows, for example, a distinct preference for the plagal cadence, for pseudo-dominant seventh-chords on the subdominant, for the type of close harmony loosely termed "barber-shop," and so on. The preference is Negroid; the chords and sequences are borrowed.

Among the borrowed elements common to the generality of hot jazz are the following:

(1) The common array of tonic, dominant and subdominant chords.

(2) Simple modulation.

(3) The typical simple European harmonic phrase which begins with a tonic chord and ends with an authentic or plagal cadence.

THE SCALAR STRUCTURE OF JAZZ

It is the simple harmonic phrase, equivalent to the stanza of European folk music, that provides the unifying principle in hot jazz improvisation. The phrase consists of a series of chords falling perhaps into as many as sixteen measures (blues melodies are usually built over a harmonic phrase of twelve measures) and arranged according to time-honored European laws of chordic sequence. This phrase is repeated over and over again, with occasional interpolations, perhaps, of other similar chordic sequences, forming a sort of "ostinato" on which the melodic and rhythmic variations are built. The form, as a whole, is not unlike that of the classical chaconne, where a chordic theme is made the subject of embellishing melodic variations. At each variation of the harmonic phrase a new melodic and rhythmic superstructure is improvised by the hot player.

Now, the hot-jazz soloist in building his melodic variations must make them accord with the prevailing harmonies of the accompaniment. A great deal of his melody is thus constructed as a sort of harmonic embellishment, and hence necessarily conforms to European scalar patterns. There is nothing essentially Negroid, for example, in the scalar structure of the following passage from the Mound City Blue Blowers recording of *You Rascal You*:

It is made up largely of *arpeggios* which merely reproduce the chords of the underlying harmony with a few incidental passing tones.

There are passages in nearly every hot improvisation, however, where the purely Negroid melodic instinct asserts itself
more fully. These occur as a rule: (1) in "breaks" where
harmony is for the moment absent; (2) in cases where the
harmonization is very Negroid in character and tends to follow,
rather than to dictate, the melody; (3) in cases (frequent in
blues) where the underlying chords are so long drawn out that
a great deal of improvisation may take place over a single
chord, free from the necessity of responding to the changes of
a complex harmonic foundation; (4) in very "dirty" hot
playing where the conventional chords of the accompaniment
are so cluttered with hectic utterances and dissonant embellishments that the details of the original harmonic phrase are
almost unrecognizable.

In these passages, despite apparent chaos, there is likely to
be a remarkable conformity of scalar elements. The improviser momentarily frees himself from the confining formulas of
the European harmonic pattern, and gives way to ecstatic
abandon. Notes are "worried" and twisted from their normal
intonation, and a number of purely Negroid scalar characteristics enter into the scheme. The result is a more authentically
"African" type of utterance, an utterance quite consistent in
its own structural peculiarities, and one whose scalar relationships may be traced (as we shall presently see) deeply into the
well-springs of racial musical habit.

That we can speak of a purely Negroid musical scale in this
connection there can be no doubt. However related to European equivalents, the pentatonic, major, minor, "gypsy" and
other scales of sweet and published Negro music may be, there
is no European precedent for the system of intonations to
which these passages of hot jazz respond.

THE SCALAR STRUCTURE OF JAZZ

In order to gain a clearer idea of the nature of this system the writer selected particularly hot passages from fourteen recordings highly regarded by swing enthusiasts, and notated them with incidental indications of pitch variation. The recordings included the following:

Wringin' and Twistin' (Tram', Bix and Lang) (Vocalion 3150).

Who? (Benny Goodman Trio) (Victor 25181-B).

Someday Sweetheart (Benny Goodman Trio) (Victor 25181-A).

Bugle Call Rag (Chocolate Dandies) (Columbia 2543-D) (151823).

Dee Blues (Chocolate Dandies) (Columbia 2543-D) (151824).

Mahogany Hall Stomp (Louis Armstrong and Orchestra) (Vocalion 3055).

Hop Off (Fletcher Henderson and Orchestra) (Brunswick 4119).

Harlemania (Duke Ellington's Orchestra) (Victor V-38045-A).

New King Porter Stomp (Fletcher Henderson and Orchestra (OKeh 41565).

Ducky Wucky (Duke Ellington) (Brunswick 6432).

Swing Low (Duke Ellington) (Brunswick 6432).

Wrappin' It Up (Fletcher Henderson and Orchestra) (Decca 157B).

Sugar Foot Strut (Louis Armstrong and his Hot Five) (OKeh 8609).

Louis Armstrong's cornet solos from *Cold in Hand Blues* (Bessie Smith) (Columbia 14064-D) (140250).

JAZZ: HOT AND HYBRID

An effort was made to exclude recordings like *You Rascal You* (Connie's Inn Orchestra) (Melotone M 12216) and *Limehouse Blues* (Fletcher Henderson) (Decca 157A) because of tricky European harmonies, or because of suspicious and very individual scalar structure in the original tune that served as a basis for improvisation. Also an attempt was made to avoid the type of recording that rests strongly on "sweet" Tin Pan Alley melodic and harmonic formulas.

The frequency of appearance of each note of the hot solos· was then carefully checked, along with its intonation and the notes that followed and preceded it. From the resulting data a table of "behavior traits" was compiled. It is unnecessary to clutter the present discussion with all the mathematical details. The process was simple enough and merely involved a check of such facts as the number of times the third degree moved to the tonic in proportion to the number of times it moved to the sixth degree, and so on.

In the process of these observations and computations a definable scale began to take shape, and certain definite traits of melodic movement began to establish themselves as universally characteristic. The tones comprising this scale may be indicated as follows:

For convenience, and because it is associated with the performance of the blues as well as with hot jazz proper, we will call it the blues scale.

Like the Doristi mode of ancient Greece,[6] and our modern

[6] See Maurice Emmanuel: Article on Greek music in the *Encyclopedia of the Paris Conservatoire*.

major scale, it consists of two similar tetrachords. Also as in the case of some of the Greek modes, each tetrachord contains a variable tone (here the third and seventh degree) which is subject to alterations in intonation. The first two tones of each tetrachord are fixed in intonation and are a whole tone apart. The fourth tone of each is also fixed in intonation and stands a perfect fourth above the first degree. The interval between the tetrachords is a major second.

The variable third tone of each tetrachord has a dual character. It may appear respectively as the third and seventh of a common major scale. Or it may take on that special character known among jazz musicians as "blue" (here indicated by a flat and a note of square shape). A "blue" note may vary in pitch by more than the scope of a half-tone. Its intonation is usually higher than that indicated by the flat before the note—*i.e.*, somewhere between flat and natural—though the player often alters its pitch during its passage, sliding up and down within the confines of this compass. A "blue" note always carries with it a curious poignant or barbaric emotional quality.

The intonation of the "blue" notes ranges, in fact, through an infinite number of gradations in pitch. This peculiarity has often been noted by commentators on Negro music. As observed earlier in this chapter, Abbe Niles, in his introduction to W. C. Handy's anthology of blues, described the tendency of the "untrained Negro voice" to "worry" these tones, "slurring and wavering between flat and natural." Krehbiel, somewhat earlier,[7] remarked that Negroes "are prone to intervallic aberrations, not only in the case of the seventh, but also in the third." The same phenomenon, as concerns the

[7] *Afro-American Folksongs*, p. 72.

seventh degree, was noted as early as 1874 by Thomas Fenner in spiritual singing by Southern Negroes. In his preface to the first edition of the *Cabin and Plantation Songs as Sung by the Hampton Students* (1874) Fenner wrote:

"Another obstacle to its [the slave music's] rendering [on paper] is the fact that tones are frequently employed which we have no musical characters to represent. Such, for example, is that which I have indicated as nearly as possible by the flat seventh in *Great Camp-Meetin', Hard Trials* and others. These tones are variable in pitch, ranging through an entire interval on different occasions, according to the inspiration of the singer. They are rarely discordant and often add a charm to the performance. It is of course impossible to explain them in words, and to those who wish to sing them the best advice is that most useful in learning to pronounce a foreign language: Study all the rules you please, then—go listen to a native."

The peculiar intonation of the seventh degree was among the phenomena that led Nicholas J. G. Ballanta-Taylor to develop a hypothesis that the Negro thinks in terms of "septimal" harmony. Ballanta-Taylor's theory seems highly speculative, and need hardly concern us here. Those interested may consult his conclusions in an unpublished monograph entitled *The Seventeen-Tone Octave,* of which mimeographed copies may be found in the library at Yaddo, Saratoga Springs, New York, in the New York Public Library, and in the Library of Congress, Washington, D. C.

The hot player adds to the diatonic blues scale a few chromatic embellishments that are common enough to deserve mention. The most familiar of these is the raised second degree used as an appoggiatura and resolving to the major third:

A well-known example of it is to be found in the following passage from Handy's *St. Louis Blues:*

The raised sixth degree, which constitutes the corresponding note of the upper tetrachord, is also used in this manner, resolving to the major seventh, though its occurrence is apparently somewhat less common. The sixth degree is also occasionally lowered by a flat and followed by the fifth. In this case the flatted tone usually serves as a passing tone between the major sixth and the fifth. All other chromatic tones are evidently uncommon, and are usually associated, when they appear, with a complex harmonic or modulative accompaniment.

Mere statement of the relative pitches of this scale, however, conveys little of its character. It is in the melodic behavior of the individual tones that its principal interest lies. And here the tetrachordal structure of the scale is convincingly demonstrated. The relationship of the two tetrachords is perhaps more clearly indicated in the following arrangement:

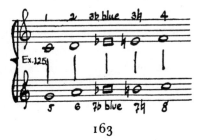

Not only are they precisely similar in structure, but the tones of each tetrachord tend to behave toward each other in very much the same way.

The first degree of the scale occupies the position of a tonic, appearing as the final note of the cadences and serving as a general center of melodic movement. In the cadences it is almost never preceded by the seventh degree, as is commonly the case in European melody. By far the most common cadential approaches are, from above by way of the blue third, and from below by way of the sixth degree. Very often the second degree appears as a passing note between the blue third and the tonic. It is interesting to note that even where the underlying harmony of a cadence consists of the standard dominant-tonic chords of European usage, the "blues" instinct of the Negro musician will bring forth a blue third or a sixth simultaneously with the dominant seventh-chord as though they were perfectly normal constituents of the dominant harmony. Occasionally the tonic will be found preceded by the fifth from below; seldom by the fifth from above. The common cadential movement centering around the tonic may be indicated, then, as follows:

The first, second and blue third degrees are the most often used notes of the lower tetrachord, and, with the addition of the sixth of the octave below, comprise the favorite tonal group of the hot jazz player. Whole melodies will be found in the simpler types of hot solo that center entirely around the tones

The blue third and the second degree, as well as the lower sixth, have a close affinity for the tonic, even in passages that are not cadential. In the vast majority of cases these tones are followed and preceded by the tonic. They are seldom found moving to and from each other without proceeding by way of the tonic. That is, while the above quoted movements and such sequences as the following

are common, it is unusual for a sixth to move to a second or a second to a third. The second degree in particular is practically always found in the immediate neighborhood of a tonic.

The *major* third degree is distinguished from the blue third both by intonation and melodic habit. Rarely the blue third may be intoned as high as the major third, but as a rule its intonation is lower, and even when it reaches that height its intonation is likely to be unstable and to slide down again. The major third, on the other hand, is definite in intonation. Used less frequently than the blue third, it serves as a general melodic component, sometimes representing the third of a tonic triad in a chord or arpeggio. Unlike the blue third it has no overwhelming affinity for the tonic and will be found moving freely upward to the fourth, fifth and sixth degrees.

Very commonly the major third is preceded by the sharped

second degree. An example of this from the *St. Louis Blues* has already been given. In a later example from the same composition, W. C. Handy follows a favorite improvisatory precedent in playing tantalizingly with the contrast between the blue third and the sharpened second degree:

Ex. 129.

This contrast is not so much a matter of intonation (on the piano the A♯ and B♭ are identical) as it is of melodic sequence and of relation to the harmonic background. The chord under the blue third (B flat) is that of the subdominant, while the B natural, following the A sharp, anticipates its own proper place as a chordic tone of the tonic triad which is the prevailing harmony of the last two measures.

The fourth degree is the least used tone of the tetrachord, and, for that matter, the least used tone of the entire scale. It is entirely lacking in a large number of hot solos. When it is found it usually has the humble place of an incidental passing tone between the third and fifth degrees, or as a chordic tone of a very important subdominant harmony. Its appearance is fairly common in such sequences as the following:

Ex. 130.

It is almost never dwelt upon except in cases where the underlying harmony begins to dominate the melodic structure.

The behavior of the upper tetrachord corresponds with

remarkable consistency to that of the lower. Its movements center about the fifth degree very much as those of the lower tetrachord center about the tonic. Its blue note (the blue seventh) behaves very much in relation to the fifth degree as the blue third behaves in relation to the tonic. Its second degree (the sixth of the scale) is closely associated with its first (the fifth of the scale) in a manner that recalls the corresponding degrees of the lower tetrachord. Thus the sequences

are among its commonest melodic movements. The tone that most commonly precedes the fifth degree of the scale is the major third of the lower tetrachord. And so we have a corresponding complex of tones around which much of the upper tessitura of hot jazz melody revolves:

If we arrange the most important tones of the scale according to tendencies of melodic movement instead of in the conventional extension from tonic to tonic, the relationship of the two tetrachordal melodic groupings becomes clearer:

Each of these two groupings shows the same arrangement of relative pitches; each centers around a "tonic" of its own toward which the other tones tend to move. The blue notes, in each case, have a downward tendency, while the lower note of each grouping tends upward toward the "tonic." Melodically the major third of the scale has a closer affinity for the upper tetrachord than for the lower, while the blue third moves solely as a component of the latter.

This is not to say, of course, that pure hot jazz melody is restricted to the confines of one or another of these groupings, without the possibility of moving between them or beyond their compasses. Certain instruments of the jazz ensemble, such as the clarinet and the saxophone, possess useful ranges of two or three octaves, and melodies played upon them extend through a broad scalar territory. But even in the most extended and florid solos—if the harmonic circumstances are such as to permit the appearance of the blues scale—little melodic whirlpools will be found continuously centering about one or the other of the tetrachordal groupings. And the simpler form of hot solo will often remain within a single grouping, or move perhaps once from the lower to the upper grouping and back again in the course of its melodic meanderings.

In the passages of hot jazz from which the above data were taken, the blue seventh had, if anything, a tendency toward slightly lower and slightly more stable intonation than the blue third. Like the blue third it often appeared simultaneously with a chord that is completely out of harmony with it according to the European notion of harmonization. Notable in this connection is its frequent appearance simultaneously with the third of the dominant seventh-chord, a note which deviates from it in intonation by as much as a half tone. The discord thus formed, which would be excruciating in European music, does not seem at all disturbing, perhaps because of the difference in tone-color between the solo and accompanying instruments. Harmonic clashes like the following

are, at any rate, not only common but highly characteristic of hot jazz structure.

There are, of course, differences in the behavior of the two tetrachords, and of their associated melodic groupings. Some of these arise from the different position each occupies in relation to the tonic of the scale. The upper tetrachord, for one thing, is somewhat less used than the lower—a not unnatural consequence of its dominant rather than tonic position. The second degree of the upper tetrachord (sixth degree of the scale) is powerfully attracted to the tonic above (the eighth scalar degree) by virtue of its position in the lower tetrachordal grouping of the octave above. This is, of course, a trait entirely lacking in the second degree of the lower tetrachord.

These, then, were the general melodic traits of the blues scale as carefully measured and checked in a considerable number of hot solos. A more cursory examination of hundreds more has shown little deviation from the principles of melodic movement we have associated with it. It may be regarded as the basic characteristic scale of jazz. Exceptions to its laws of intonation and movement naturally occur. Notes other than the blue notes are frequently subject to distortions of intonation, particularly by jazz trumpeters. I have even heard the theory of a "blue fifth" advanced, though I have never been able to find any consistent evidence to support such a theory. Extremely "dirty" hot playing is liable to produce any amount of wild distortion. But even in this sort of jazz, the most consistent intonations and sequences—the ones that occur over and over again and stamp the music with its fundamental melodic character—are the ones we have noted here.

It is undoubtedly this blues scale—which appears so consistently in hot jazz, and which we will presently trace to more sober and venerable sources—that forms the basis of the "blue" melodies of Tin Pan Alley. The published blues of W. C. Handy follow it pretty closely, though more elaborate harmonizations and modulations cause some natural departures from primitive simplicity.

Musical notation is, of course, incapable of expressing the precise intonations of the blue notes, and the customary compromise is merely a scale with a flat third and a flat seventh. The piano, with its fixed intonation, is likewise limited to compromises where these deviations from conventional pitch are concerned. One of these compromises has been permanently imbedded in the tradition of jazz pianism. It consists of striking the flat and natural third simultaneously:

For convenience in notation the flat third is usually indicated enharmonically as the sharped second (here G♯ instead of A♭). The resulting blurred effect at least symbolizes the wavering intonation it is supposed to represent. At any rate it became very popular among jazz pianists and spread from the blues accompaniments where it originated to all sorts of jazz.

Aside from, or notwithstanding such tricks of jazz pianism, the average Tin Pan Alley tune, with what we might call added "bluing," has been a comparatively conventional affair. The use of flat thirds and sevenths in popular tunes is a venerable one, probably antedating considerably the commercial advent of the blues proper.

The typical Tin Pan Alley "blues" tune is perhaps as well represented as anywhere in the melody of Roy Turk's *Beale Street Mama:*

In this simple phrase are to be noted, at *a* the natural third of the scale followed by the common sequence of second and first degrees; at *b* the typical sequence of the sharped second degree and the major third; at *c* the flatted (blue) seventh; at *d* the notational equivalent of the blue third moving, according to rule, through the second degree to the tonic; and finally the typical cadence where the tonic is approached through the sixth degree of the lower octave. Note also how in the last four bars the melodic movement revolves around the following tones

the same lower-tetrachord group that we have found to be so favored in the melodies of the hot improvisers.

Chapter 10

THE DERIVATION OF THE BLUES

THE WIDESPREAD USE of the blues scale in commercial jazz apparently started with the rise in popularity of the blues around 1914. Its influence, as we have already seen, was largely responsible for putting a final period to the age of the piano rag. The influence was by no means limited to the "blues" proper, a form which, at the time, was being widely exploited by W. C. Handy and other composers of sheet music. It began to permeate the melodic contours and harmonic chord sequences of half the music turned out by Tin Pan Alley, even when this music was not supposed to be Negroid. It became deeply imbedded in the style of popular Broadway composers like Gershwin. It added a new, permanent ingredient to the American popular musical language.

As to the blues proper, they constituted a special autonomous form of jazz, just as the piano rag had before them. The harmonic details of the blues will be considered in another chapter. The most striking feature of the form was a twelve-bar phraseology which set it apart from the eight- and sixteen-bar phraseology of all other popular music. The blues stanza, so to speak, was a three-line instead of a four-line stanza; and this was something new in the prosody of Western popular music.

The blues were, of course, sung and played long before they

became a popular feature of commercial music. Negro musicians like "Jelly Roll" Morton were singing them in New Orleans shortly after the turn of the century. And they were probably sung on the levees and in the cotton fields long before that. Because of their deviations from standard intonation, they cannot be adequately studied, like the piano rag, from published sheet music. Handy's famous blues, for example, are almost never sung as they appear in print—at least not by the best Negro blues singers. In order to trace the scale structure of the blues as sung, rather than as printed, I have made use of several recordings of the late Bessie Smith, a singer whose improvisations on the tunes of Handy and others show the Negroid vocal style in its purest form. Almost any musically sensitive person—even one who is not partial to jazz— will admit that her recordings of *Cold in Hand Blues* (Columbia 14064-D) and the venerable ditty *You've Been a Good Ole Wagon, but You Done Broke Down* (Columbia 14079-D) are musical experiences of a high and poetic order.

Bessie Smith's style represents a conceded standard of excellence in the art of blues declamation. It is both somewhat simpler and somewhat more purely "African" than the style of the average blues singer. She uses a very small range and a very limited scale. *Cold in Hand Blues,* for example, rests almost entirely on a scale of four notes. However complex the harmony underlying her vocal melody, she changes her scalar pattern only rarely and slightly by way of compromise with it. Often her tones do not "harmonize" with the chords of the accompaniment according to the European notion of harmonization. But the sureness and consistency of her deviations from European usage carry with them their own artistic justification. And the effect is undeniably satisfactory. Her treatment of conventional blues tunes is exceedingly free, in the sense that she pays very little attention to the notes, or even the words, of the printed version. As in the case of all true "hot" soloists, the rigid conventional lines of the standard tune on which her improvisation is based often become almost unrecognizable in what she produces. Her freedom of treatment, however, is not the freedom of elaboration. She does not add florid elements to the original tune. She rather subtracts its superfluous elements, pruning it down and simplifying its phraseology; making it, in fact, more truly "primitive."

The scale employed by Bessie Smith is the one we have described as the blues scale, and she uses it with a degree of purity rarely attained in the more florid flights of instrumental jazz. Most of her songs are based on a single tetrachordal grouping, either the upper or the lower, and strayings beyond the four-note limits of this grouping are infrequent.

You've Been a Good Ole Wagon is sung almost entirely on the four tones of the lower tetrachordal grouping:

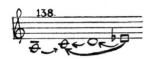

Two of these notes bear the principal burdens of her melodic line—the tonic (C) and the blue third degree, with indefinite and wavering intonation. The latter tone is often used simultaneously with the tonic chord of her accompaniment, and, of course, clashes violently with its major third. This clash, however, does not seem to disturb her in the least.

You've Been a Good Ole Wagon, Copyright M. Witmark & Sons. Used by permission.

The song consists of a single stanza, stated and repeated three times with considerable variation in the vocal part. The following is an approximation, in musical notation, of the first stanza. A simplified indication of the harmony is given to show how the chordic structure affects the melodic line.

THE DERIVATION OF THE BLUES

Bessie Smith's intonation for the blue third differs considerably in different places and is indicated here by the square notehead and either a flat or a natural, depending on which most closely approximates it at the moment. Where the deviation is markedly distant from either, an arrow above the note indicates its direction. In most cases, however, the deviation lies somewhere between flat and natural, seldom descending below the conventional tempered pitch here indicated as E flat.

Typical are the appearances of the blue third simultaneously with the major third (E natural) of the tonic triad in measures 1, 2 and 3; and the appearance of the same tone as seventh of a pseudo-dominant seventh-chord on the subdominant

in measures 5 and 6. This cool freedom with which European conceptions of melody are disregarded is both amazing and refreshing. Note also how closely Bessie Smith sticks to her tetrachordal grouping of four tones. An added G in the first and in the second-from-the-last measures seems to be the only deviation not accounted for by harmonic influences.

In the last half of the stanza several factors conspire against the simplicity of scalar treatment. The underlying harmony modulates temporarily to the relative minor, and then a passage in "barbershop" harmony, involving a chromatic sequence of seventh-chords, brings in the original key again. In spite of this, however, it is remarkable how slightly the singer deviates from her original tetrachordal series. In measure 9 a clear major third (E natural) appears as the fifth of the new key; yet in measure 11 this brave new fifth, in a corresponding position, becomes violently blue in intonation— so much so, in fact, that it is difficult to tell where it is natural, where flat and where it most clearly approximates the second degree of the scale. As far as the scale of the melody is concerned the only indications of a change of key are the somewhat greater prominence of the sixth degree, and the clear consistent intonation of the major third in measure 9. The scalar manifestations of measures 13 and 14 are largely dictated by the rapidly shifting harmony of the piano part.

Where *You're Been a Good Ole Wagon* occupies exclusively the lower tetrachordal grouping of tones, the *Cold in Hand Blues* is sung entirely in the grouping associated with the upper tetrachord. Whether the singer herself was conscious of this change of orientation in relation to the tonic may be questioned, although she uses her scalar material somewhat differently in the new surroundings. The actual pitches of her tones may, of course, be the same in both recordings, and the change may have been brought about by a shift in the key of the accompaniment. At any rate, in relation to a theoretically stable tonic (assumed here for convenience to be the note C); the chief tones used in *Cold in Hand Blues* are the following:

141.

The principal melodic burden is borne this time by the fifth and sixth degrees (G and A). The blue seventh appears less frequently than did the third blue of *You've Been a Good Ole Wagon,* and when it does appear it is usually accompanied by a dominant harmony. The third scalar degree (E) here also assumes a melodic role that is somewhat different from

178

that of its corresponding note (the sixth degree) in the lower tetrachordal grouping. In this song it seems to be associated always with the final chord of each phrase, where it becomes the third of the tonic triad. This is an approximation of the "verse" and of one stanza of the repeated "chorus" that follows:

Ex. 142.

Ah've got a hard work-in' man, The way he treats me I can't un-der-stan' He works hard ev-ry day, an' on

The intonation of the blue seventh, as in the case of the blue third of *You've Been a Good Ole Wagon,* is, as a rule, somewhat higher than the flat and somewhat lower than the natural seventh of European custom. The blue seventh is usually accompanied here by the dominant seventh-chord. There is, of course, a clash between it and the third of the dominant chord, but it seems to disturb neither the listener nor the singer.

Bessie Smith's version of the famous *St. Louis Blues* is governed more by complicated harmonic considerations than either of the above mentioned recordings. Handy's composition contains a section in the minor scale—an unusual feature in the simpler type of blues—and there are other factors of a chordic nature that tend to force the singer into more sophisticated scalar treatment. Nevertheless it is interesting to note that the vocal interpretation tends always to simplify rather than to complicate Handy's original melody. In the sections that are major (or blue) in modality she reduces Handy's rather chromatic scalar material

to the primitive series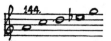

which corresponds exactly to the lower blues tetrachordal grouping of *You've Been a Good Ole Wagon* plus an upper fifth degree. Handy's

(here given in the original key of the notated version) becomes
Bessie Smith's

Ah hate to see the evenin' sun go down.

Handy's

becomes

Bessie Smith's

Ex. 148. Feel-in' to-mor-row lax Ah feel to-day.

In this recording the intonation of the blue third is generally
lower instead of higher than the conventional flatted third of
European usage. The second degree of the scale here also
tends to be sung off pitch, and it is often difficult to distinguish second from third degree. As in *You've Been a Good
Ole Wagon* (despite these differences in intonation) the blue
third appears, in the major sections, over tonic, dominant and
subdominant harmonies.

*   *   *   *   *

Bessie Smith's melodic style undoubtedly reflects the influence of a deep-rooted racial musical instinct. While comparatively few of the published spirituals show with any clarity
these completely un-European melodic habits we have been
describing, a great deal of primitive Southern spiritual singing

actually follows them with remarkable consistency. Where the trained and self-conscious Negro chorus is more likely to imitate European or "white" constructions, the little rural congregations of the Deep South, raising their voices in spontaneous religious communion, often drone their more fervent outbursts in the intervals of the blues tetrachords. Even when the medium is speech rather than song, as in sermons and prayers, the blues intonations creep into the texture of their discourse. The Negro preacher will commence his sermon in a matter-of-fact voice, stressing his words carefully so as to convey with the utmost clarity the logic of his thought. As he and his congregation warm to their common devotional task, however, his intonations will begin to crystallize, and soon a frenzy of religious ecstasy will be reached in which his speech becomes a recitative with clearly defined musical values. Very commonly the ecstatic part of such a sermon will be found to rest, melodically, on two or three notes of a blues tetrachord. One sermon, recorded by E. P. Jennings in central Alabama, is sung—or "preached" if you like—entirely on two notes: a tonic, or main declamatory tone, and the "blue" third above it. Both congregation and preacher echo each other frequently in snatches like

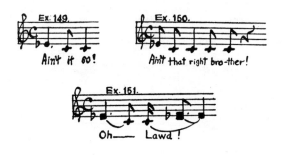

Some of the preacher's phrases, interspersed with punctuating grunts, possess not only well-defined musical intonation, but even musical rhythm in which polyrhythmic formations are to be clearly distinguished. A long discourse on the conversion of Paul brings forth many phrases like the following: [1]

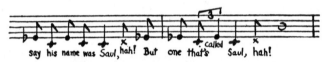

In the more crystallized form of religious singing among these congregations the use of the blues tetrachords is, naturally, somewhat more elaborate. The primitive recording of the spiritual *John Saw de Number*, also recorded by E. P. Jennings, shows the blue tetrachordal earmarks clearly:

[1] Compare the polyrhythmic construction with measures 3 and 4 of Bessie Smith's *You've Been a Good Ole Wagon*.

THE DERIVATION OF THE BLUES

The spiritual *Nora, Nora,* quoted earlier, shows similar melodic tendencies, particularly striking in the recurrent phrase: [2]

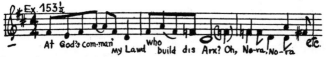

At God's com-man My Lawd who build dis Arx? Oh, No-ra, No-ra

Just where song begins and speech leaves off, however, is a difficult point to establish in the primitive ceremonies of the South. Spirituals like the foregoing may reach a somewhat more definite musical crystallization than sermons or prayers. But the wealth of musical elements attending a really fervent bit of Negro religious oratory is often nearly as striking as that associated with the spirituals themselves. To illustrate this point more fully the writer is led to quote at some length an improvised prayer transcribed approximately in musical notation from another recording in the possession of E. P. Jennings. As a demonstration of the deep-rooted place occupied by the blues scale in the musical consciousness of the Negro it is striking. The speaker uses the entire tonal group associated with the blues tetrachord and reaches above it on two or three ecstatic occasions for the fifth degree of the scale. The complete group of tones on which he bases his incantation is the following:

Here and there the transcriber has had recourse to symbols not ordinarily used in musical notation. The stems minus note-heads represent an ordinary conversational tone of voice, usually much lower than the intonations of the fixed group of

---

[2] Measure 2 here contains similarity of scalar structure to the first measure (quoted above) of Bessie Smith's version of the *St. Louis Blues.*

declamatory tones. Now and then, especially where the blue third is concerned, an arrow above the note indicates a particularly large deviation from the pitch shown, either up or down. A parenthesis around a note indicates that it is very faint in volume. The blue third is symbolized, as in previous examples, by a square note-head.

The rhythm is that of free prose, and, of course, is only vaguely approximated in musical notation. Bar lines have been omitted as superfluous. The declamation falls naturally into short phrases between each of which there is a pause. In a few places where the text is so obscured by the surrounding exclamations of the congregation as to be indistinguishable in the recording, dashes are given in place of syllables.

[3] The material deleted showed no scalar differences from that quoted.

The appearance of the blues tetrachords in primitive spiritual singing and even in Afro-American prose declamation should convince the most skeptical of their authenticity as a characteristic Negroid contribution. Regarding the pentatonic and other supposedly Negroid scalar constructions there is legitimate room for controversy. These constructions are common to the folk idioms of several races, and there is some possibility that they have been borrowed by the Negro. But the blues scale is his own unique product, and its use in American popular music is to be traced directly to his influence.

THE DERIVATION OF THE BLUES

That the Afro-American has intoned this scale since the earliest days of slavery can hardly be doubted. The earliest reference to it in print that this writer has come across is the remark of Thomas P. Fenner quoted previously. But its widespread appearance in all sorts of Negro declamation, as well as in the singing of spirituals whose origin is demonstrably at least three generations behind us, suggests a far more venerable pedigree. It is patently impossible for the Negro to have borrowed it. The whites did not use it, nor has any scalar construction similar to it been used in European music for many centuries.

Chapter 11

HARMONY

THE ANALYSIS of jazz harmony offers a different problem from that involved in our surveys of rhythm and scale. The harmonic structure of jazz is by far its least Negroid aspect. Harmony as it is used in jazz and in the published spirituals is basically a European principle. We cannot speak here of the fusion of similar elements in two different musical idioms. What Negroid elements there are in jazz harmonization arise from the effect of Negro taste, and of Negro melodic habit, upon a structural method that remains essentially White, or European.

Controversy as to whether the African Negro does or does not "think in terms of harmony" has gone on for some time. It has been pointed out that some native African music has definite polyphonic characteristics. "With all due allowance for White influence [in the spirituals], which has been great, of course," writes Natalie Curtis-Burlin, in her *Hampton Series of Negro Folk-Songs* (Book 2, p. 7), "the fact remains that in savage Africa, remote from European culture, many of the most primitive pagan songs are sung in parts with elaborate interludes on drums tuned to different pitches. Indeed, the music of the Dark Continent is rich in polyphonic as well as in rhythmic suggestions for the European." Subsequent ethnological research has, in fact, confirmed her statement. But a lack of precise definition here tends to cloud the issue. Harmony as used in jazz, spirituals, blues and most types of hot improvisation consists of orderly arrangements of chords based upon what are indisputably long-established European laws of sequence. These chords and sequences, which form a part of the technique of "harmony" as Europeans know it, are utterly foreign to the music of Africa. That the native African may sing and drum polyphonically after a method of his own, does not alter the case. The system of harmonization used by the American Negro is not the African system, but a simplified and characteristic dialect of the European system.

There is no denying, however, that the Negroes of our South possess an uncanny ability to improvise collectively in the White man's harmonic system; that, in fact, they will often put the White man to shame in the use of his own materials when it comes to creating on the spur of the moment. "One has but to attend a colored church, whether North or South," writes Mrs. Curtis-Burlin in the same connection, "to hear men and women break naturally into alto, tenor or bass parts (and even subdivisions of these), to realize how instinctively the Negro musical mind thinks harmonies." Part singing, instinctive with the Negro or not, comes very naturally to him, and his feeling for the European sequences is remarkable. One need only reflect upon the preponderantly harmonic character of the music—jazz, spirituals and so on—in which the Negro has had a hand, to realize how important harmony has become in his musical consciousness. Spirituals without harmony are comparatively rare; jazz without harmony is unthinkable.

As far as variety of chords is concerned, the harmonization of the general run of published spirituals is very simple. Few of them venture beyond the tonic, dominant and subdominant triads, and the dominant seventh-chord. Some of them are limited to one or two of these, the subdominant triad being often preferred to the dominant harmonies.

This choice of chords is the same as that upon which the great majority of White hymn tunes, and indeed of most Anglo-Celtic folk music, is based. Even the apparent preference for subdominant and plagal harmony can hardly be spoken of as Negroid here, though the same preference forms a striking feature of blues harmonization. Subdominant and plagal harmonies have always been common in the church music of the Whites. In the spirituals an added reason for the frequency of the plagal cadence is to be found in the fact that so many of them approach their final tonic by way of the sixth degree from below, a note which invites subdominant harmonization.

As a whole then, harmony in the published spirituals cannot be said to display any very striking Negroid characteristics. Where the transcription has been very scrupulous, as in the case of Natalie Curtis-Burlin's and Ballanta-Taylor's versions, there is evident a natural feeling for sonority and smooth voice leading and a tendency to disregard such classical European niceties as the prohibition against consecutive octaves and fifths. But it is none the less evident that the Negro is using a borrowed structural principle, and using it very much as his preceptors do.

Undoubtedly the sophisticated harmonization of the "concert" spiritual has assisted in the expulsion of many typically Negroid elements from this type of composition. Nathaniel Dett, in the *Religious Folksongs of the Negro* [1] has quoted two versions of the spiritual *Roll, Jordan, Roll*, one transcribed from the singing of Hampton Institute students a half century

[1] Hampton Institute Press, 1927.

ago, the other transcribed at the same institution just prior to 1927. The difference between the two is both striking and significant. The earlier version shows clearly the traces of blues scalar structure, containing the flatted "blue" seventh and exhibiting several quite un-European habits of melodic movement. In the latter version both melody and harmony have become more standardized according to White usage. The harmonically embarrassing blue seventh has been done away with, a White plagal "semi-cadence" has been introduced halfway through the first phrase, and the general melodic contour has been brought into line with European convention. Mr. Dett ascribes these changes to metaphysical sources, believing that the modern version reflects the greater ease of present-day life among the Negroes. It is quite obvious, however, that the dominating force in these changes is the influence of the White man's harmonic system. A typically Negroid tune has, in the hands of educated and artistically conscious Negroes, been gradually divested of its primitive character and endowed with the standardized physiognomy of a White hymn. Who can say how many of the popular spirituals have undergone a similar change? In the end not much is left of the typically Negroid characteristics. It is especially interesting to note in connection with this example, that while the modern version is predominantly pentatonic in scale-structure, the older and more purely Negroid version is not at all pentatonic and leans strongly toward the intonations of the blues scale.

While there is reason to believe that a certain sacrifice of primitive Negroid elements has attended the development of most harmonized "concert" spirituals, it is also apparent that the primitive Negro of the "hot" spiritual, and other types of quasi-musical religious expression, employs harmony only in a very rudimentary manner. Whether such "harmony" has been developed by imitation of white musical customs or whether it may properly be described as "African" is open to question. The circumstances of mass improvisation by whole congregations lend themselves somewhat naturally to a many-voiced type of expression. The technique used by primitive congregations, however, hardly qualifies as "harmony" in the European sense of the term, nor does it apparently bear much relation to the harmonic structure of hot jazz, blues, or other more complex and White-influenced varieties of Negroid music.

In such examples of primitive Negro religious improvisation as have been heard by the present writer "harmony" has been limited to tones of the pentatonic and blues scales, and the simultaneous combinations of these tones have occurred fortuitously and without apparent design.[2] The result is not unpleasing to the ear. The tones of these scales combine fairly readily, especially in purely vocal music, and there is something of primitive vitality in the sound of a large number of voices singing simultaneous melodies based on them. But such "harmony" lacks entirely the element of *progression* from chord to chord that is all-important to harmonic form in the European sense. Thus, pure Negro polyphony would appear to be merely the accidental result of varying Negroid intonations being sung at the same time by large groups of singers. This sort of polyphony is rich in pure Negro elements, but can hardly be termed "harmonic," as Europeans understand it.

In reshaping and fitting this sort of polyphony to the tonic, dominant and subdominant formulas of European custom, the

[2] For a somewhat similar harmonic use of scalar materials by the native Africans, see pp. 217–219.

Negro pays with a loss of many native peculiarities. This fact undoubtedly goes a long way to explain the rarity of blues scalar constructions in the published spirituals. In the more popular fields of Negroid musical expression, however, the process has been to a certain extent reversed. While the White man's harmony has dominated the Negro's intonations in the "concert" spiritual, the Negro's intonations in hot jazz and in the blues have dominated, or at least deeply affected, the White man's system of harmony.

A simple example of this Negro influence on White harmonic formula will be found in the structure of the conventional blues. The usual blues tune is made up of twelve-bar phrases, one or two such phrases sufficing, with appropriate repetitions, for the entire composition. Harmonically, the structure of these phrases is highly conventional, most blues conforming to a basic pattern that admits only of slight variation. The pattern is notable for the large number of seventh-chords employed, and for a propensity to swing back and forth between tonic and subdominant harmonies. If we employ the common symbols I, V and IV for tonic, dominant and subdominant harmonies respectively, as well as the designation 7 for a seventh-chord (always formed like a dominant seventh-chord, with two minor thirds standing above a major third) we can designate this pattern approximately as follows:

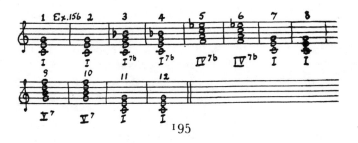

JAZZ: HOT AND HYBRID

This type of harmonic pattern, with pseudo-dominant seventh-chords on the subdominant, is unknown among the simpler song accompaniments of Europe. It is a distinctly original grouping of European harmonies. Two seventh-chords found only rarely (and usually in a highly sophisticated context) in European music, are used here––a pseudo-dominant seventh-chord built on the tonic, and another pseudo-dominant seventh-chord built on the subdominant. Each of these chords may be traced directly to the influence of the blues scale. Each involves a chromatic note foreign to the European major scale. These chromatic notes alter the third and seventh degrees, respectively, of the European major scale, those degrees whose flatted "blue" quality makes them the earmarks of the Negro's characteristic tonal series. The blue tones here are represented by B flat and E flat. The chords

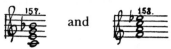

are derived, not from our major scale, but from the scale

which we have found to be so inextricably connected with the racial musical instincts of the Negro.

Naturally where the piano is the accompanying instrument the characteristic wavering intonation of these tones does not appear. The Negro does, however, make use of blues intonations as components of chords when his instrumental or vocal means permit. Those interested in the peculiar flavor imparted to a chordic sequence when its blue notes are given

HARMONY

their Negroid deviations in pitch will find remarkable examples of this phenomenon in the recordings of Mitchell's Christian Singers, notably in the spiritual *What More Can Jesus Do?* which we have already quoted in other connections.

The importance of harmony as a controlling structural principle in jazz has been hinted at in our chapter on scale. It is the harmonic pattern of a jazz tune that provides the foundation upon which the hot jazz improviser builds his spontaneous variations. This pattern, in the vast bulk of hot jazz improvisations, conforms to one or another of a half-dozen simple formulas. Sometimes it is taken bodily from the accompaniment of one of the large number of Tin Pan Alley tunes which also conform to these formulas. Elsewhere it may be spontaneously created by the players. But the word "spontaneously" here must be taken as indicating merely the fact that printed music is not used or referred to. The harmonic patterns of hot jazz do not vary as do its melodies. They are quite conventional, and are used over and over again, serving as the accompaniments of one tune after another. In "re-creating" them the hot player is merely repeating a time-honored formula, even though what he does has the appearance of an improvisatory process.

Jazz harmonization, in what we might call its metropolitan form, presents a bewildering mixture of idioms and influences. The composers and arrangers of Tin Pan Alley use today, in their more sophisticated accompaniments, a harmonic language that stems as much from Wagner and Puccini as it does from American, Negro-influenced sources. If we set such refinements aside for the moment, however, we will find that the bread-and-butter basis of jazz harmonization exhibits the influence of two very important musical factors. The first of these is the type of close chromatic harmony known as "barbershop." The second is our old friend the blues scale.

"Barbershop" harmony has been associated with American hillbilly and cowboy music, with theatrical "male quartets," with various types of Negroid music and with barroom conviviality, for many decades at least. Perhaps its most familiar appearance to most of us is in the harmony that is customarily associated with the mournful song *Sweet Adeline,* sung in chorus. It is said that it originated in the barbershops of the South, where, to while away the time on hot afternoons, barbers, tonsorial subjects and waiting customers would blend their voices in "harmonizing" a current tune or so. However that may be, "barbershop" harmony does possess a particular physiognomy of its own which distinguishes it from the simpler forms of European harmonization.

In "barbershop" harmony the voices tend to stick close together and to move in parallel formations. As often as possible the movement is by chromatic half-steps. Seventh- and ninth-chords are as common as, if not more common than, triads—especially seventh- and ninth-chords of "dominant" formation. These latter often succeed each other by parallel chromatic movement, and by such cyclical progression through related keys as the following:

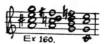

Ex 160.

In the more sophisticated developments of jazz harmonization these chromatic and cylical progressions of seventh-chords may have provided a natural link with, or a natural springboard to, the use of Wagnerian types of chordic structure

HARMONY

and movement. They represent, at any rate, a type of harmonic structure that was at least exceptional in European music until the time of Liszt and Wagner. That the hillbillies and other rural songsters of America learned the trick from the masterpieces of the German romanticists is highly unlikely. Nor does this particular style of harmonization show any definite Negroid qualities, though the Negroes have undoubtedly used it. More likely is it that the chromatic peculiarities of "barbershop" arose indirectly from the structural character of accompanying instruments like banjo and guitar.

These instruments are so constructed as to encourage the use of chords of three or more notes, each chord being produced by a certain arrangement of the fingers of the left hand. Once such a chord as the dominant seventh had been memorized and its peculiar fingering established as a habit, it would be rather natural for the player to seek to use the same finger arrangement at other points of the scale. The process, mechanically, would simply amount to moving the hand up or down the neck of the instrument while retaining the same relative positions of the fingers. Working by trial and error our hypothetical banjoist would find that his dominant-seventh finger arrangement clicked at certain levels with given points of a tune, and gave him a useful added resource in harmonizing. It is easy to see how this process might have evolved the common practice of substituting a chromatic pseudo-dominant seventh-chord on the lowered sixth degree for the subdominant triad in the cadence:

The fingerings of the first two chords on a banjo or similar instrument would be identical. The progression between them

199

would be accomplished merely by moving the hand one fret
lower on the fingerboard. Thus, probably, did rural America
first acquaint itself with the mysteries of post-Wagnerian chromaticism. One need only listen to a college boy strumming a
ukulele to find the process exhibited.

Now, "barbershop" harmony has contributed a great deal
to the technique of jazz harmonization. It is to blame for
much of the popularity that seventh- and ninth-chords enjoy
in the jazz accompanist's scheme of things, as well as for his
love of parallel movement, and of chromatic smoothness in
the progression of individual voices. Sequences like these

(quoted from the accompaniment of Bessie Smith's *You've
Been a Good Ole Wagon*) involve a degree of chromaticism
never reached in the folk tunes of Europe. Yet they have been
an elementary commonplace in the rural American art of song
accompaniment for many years.

From "barbershop" harmony jazz adopted the formula of
moving from dominant seventh to dominant seventh, or ninth,
through cycles of related keys. This formula is now used so
incessantly in Tin Pan Alley accompaniments that it qualifies
as a jazz characteristic. Modulation is not really involved.
The formula is used continuously in "breaks" like the following

where it serves as a momentary distraction from the sameness
of key. It also appears in the main body of two out of every
three sheet-music accompaniments. I quote here, as an example, the chorus of Ted Fiorito's and Ernie Erdman's *No,
No, Nora*. The entire phrase, like hundreds of its kind, is
built upon a cycle of dominant seventh-chords resolving to
other dominant seventh-chords:

With incidental embellishments left out, the chordic series here corresponds to this simplified formula

which is typical "barbershop."

The "barbershop" preference for seventh-chords over simple triads has been taken over with a vengeance by the jazz composers. In jazz harmonization one can almost say that the seventh- or ninth-chord is the rule; the triad the exception. Where the more sophisticated type of sheet-music accompaniment is concerned, one often has to search measure after measure before finding even so important a representative of the species as the plain tonic triad. Here it is fairly common for a tune to begin on the dominant seventh-chord of its dominant's dominant, or on some other harmony equally distant from its own key center, and to work toward its tonic through a series of chromatic harmonies, reaching it perhaps only in the final cadence. Such cases constitute, however, extreme refinements of the "barbershop" principle, and are not often found where jazz is of the hot variety.

*　　*　　*　　*　　*

The purely Negroid influence in jazz harmonization is most evident in those cases where the European harmonic scheme has been affected by the melodic peculiarities of the blues scale. And these cases are by no means limited to the blues proper. One of the most striking differences between jazz harmonization and conventional European harmonization lies in the handling of cadences. By far the commonest cadence in European harmonization consists of the dominant seventh-chord and its resolution to the tonic triad. This is the so-called *authentic* cadence. Next in order of importance is the *plagal* cadence, in which the subdominant triad precedes the final tonic chord. In jazz the authentic and plagal cadences are used comparatively seldom; seldom, that is, in the pure, unadorned forms which serve for the bulk of European harmonizations. The reasons for this will be found in the influences exerted over them by the Negroid blues scale.

As has been remarked in the chapter on scale, jazz seldom employs the "leading tone," or rising seventh degree, of European melody. In Negroid melody (as well as in all jazz, which here shows an important Negro influence) the final note of a tune is usually preceded from above (1) by the major or minor (blue) third; (2) by the major or minor third followed by the second; or, from below, by the sixth degree of the scale. These typical melodic endings

coincide with the principle of melodic movement peculiar to the blues tetrachordal grouping:

The penultimate chord of the jazz cadence thus has to conform, harmonically, to the major or minor third, the second or the sixth degree of the scale. Of these tones, only the second harmonizes with the dominant triad or seventh-chord of European custom. This situation has brought about the use of a number of chords, uncommon in European cadences, which combine the Negroid melodic characteristics of the blues scale with the appropriate feeling of finality. Most of these may be regarded as alterations of the authentic and plagal forms. But they are quite typical of and peculiar to jazz.

The commonest cadences in jazz are probably the following:

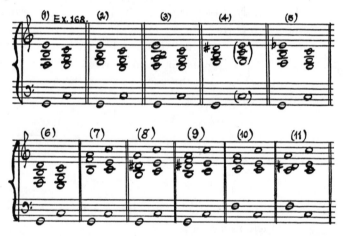

They have been arranged here according to the melodic movement of the upper voice; the first six (No. 4 has exceptional uses) are used as descending, the last five as ascending cadences. No. 6 is the conventional authentic cadence of European harmonization, which is often used in descending cadences, but can hardly be said to hold a dominating place in the jazz scheme of things. No. 10 is the common European plagal cadence. No. 4 is the augmented triad on the dominant which often remains unresolved at the end of a "verse," creating an atmosphere of expectancy for the initial tonic harmonies of the "chorus" which is to follow. No. 5, with its E flat changed enharmonically to D sharp, often fulfills a similar function. All of these, except perhaps No. 4 are especially adapted to fit the cadential peculiarities of the blues scale. And so important have these peculiarities become in the jazz idiom that it is only very rarely that a jazz tune or accompanying cadential figure fails to respect them. This phenomenon holds true from the most spontaneous swing music to the most standardized products of Tin Pan Alley.

That these typical cadences of jazz originated in the accompaniment of Negro melody is obvious if one glances at the Bessie Smith transcriptions in the preceding chapter. This singer's use of the blue third simultaneously with the dominant seventh-chord has already been commented on. The resultant combination (which some might refer to as a chord of the dominant thirteenth) is undoubtedly the prototype of the initial chord in cadences 1 and 5 above. At the end of measure 6 of the *You've Been a Good Ole Wagon* transcription on p. 176 (and at several subsequent points in the same recording) will be found the prototype of cadence 7 above. Cadences 8 and 9 are variants of cadence 7 employing the blue third (here enharmonically converted from E flat to D sharp). Cadence 10 is the plagal cadence favored in the published spirituals and in much other Negroid music. Cadence 11 uses the pseudo-dominant seventh-chord on the subdominant, which is so characteristic of blues harmonization, as its penultimate. (Here again the white man's laws of progression, and Tin Pan Alley custom, cause us to change the E flat enharmonically to D sharp.) Thus have Negro melody and White harmony combined to influence the harmonic dialect of jazz.

There are other ways, too, in which the blues scale has influenced the conventional pattern of jazz harmonization. The blue third, with its indefinite intonation and its habit of moving downward through the second degree to the tonic, has created a whole set of characteristic figures. Some of these have already been referred to as elements peculiar to jazz pianism. While the blue third, intoned high enough, coincided pretty well with the more diatonic "barbershop" progression

Ex. 169.

its lower intonation demanded such chromatic and "blue" "barbershop" progressions as

Ex. 170.   and   Ex. 171.

The same relation between blue third and second degrees is undoubtedly to blame for the little figure

which will be found embellishing the dominant seventh-chord in nearly every Tin Pan Alley accompaniment. More elaborate versions of the same figure like

have been exploited by such sophisticates as Gershwin. A reverse movement of the blues tones contributed to the pianistic "blues" figure

so beloved by Zez Confrey. It is the flat and natural approximations of the blue third that provide the colorful elements in the following typical extended cadential figure by Confrey (*Modern Course in Novelty Piano Playing*, p. 21):

207

JAZZ: HOT AND HYBRID

The unstable Negro intonation is represented by the simultaneous F sharp and G of measure 1, the simultaneous F natural and F sharp and following G at the beginning of measure 2, and by the G flat in the chromatic "barbershop" chord at the end of measure 2.

*   *   *   *   *

The characteristics of jazz harmonization that we have outlined here all entered the field of popular sheet music with the advent of the blues. It is, in fact, they, rather than the supposed and much-talked-about rhythmic distinctions, that constitute the main difference between jazz and ragtime. The harmony of the latter art seldom contained evidences of Negro influence, or even of "barbershop" construction. Ragtime held, by and large, to the conventions of the simpler type of European harmonic phraseology, resting securely on the tonic, dominant and subdominant harmonies common alike to *Annie Laurie, O Sole Mio* and *Ach du Lieber Augustin.*

Jazz then is, as a whole, more Negroid than ragtime, and is so largely because of the presence of important Negro influences in its harmony. Aside from the Wagner-Puccini-Impressionist conceits of the sophisticated Tin Pan Alleyites, jazz harmonization is affected from two clearly defined sources: "barbershop" harmony, and the blues scale. Of these, the latter at least is a purely Negroid contribution.

As to the differences between the harmonic aspects of hot jazz and those of Tin Pan Alley jazz, they are not as great as might be imagined. Hot jazz harmony in general is probably simpler than Tin Pan Alley harmony. The sophisticated European ingredients are less likely to be found in it; and it is more likely to stick to a few elementary "barbershop" and blues formulas. One must, however, remember in this connection that the improvisatory elements that add so much color to the melodic and rhythmic aspects of hot jazz are not to be found in the harmonic field. Apart from a certain freedom of variation in ornamental pianistic figures, hot jazz harmonization is not improvisatory, but, on the contrary, is highly standardized. Here and there, when a Tin Pan Alley tune is being used for improvisation, the sophisticated elements of the original harmonization will pervade the hot version. *Limehouse Blues*, for example, begins on a chromatically altered seventh chord whose root is in the sixth degree of the scale. This tricky harmony is used by hot ensembles throughout their "improvised" variations on the tune. It is not, however, a typically Negroid construction, and does not appear elsewhere in the general run of hot jazz accompaniments. It is simply a sophisticated characteristic of this rather sophisticated piece, and as such has been taken over by the musicians who use it as a basis for hot improvisation.

The great bulk of hot jazz, on the other hand, conforms harmonically to the simpler standard habits of jazz accompaniment. Its melodies and rhythms find their most congenial development over harmonic substructures in which the blues influence is strong. The blues patterns quoted earlier in this chapter have done yeoman service as basic formulas for hot jazz accompaniments. Other common formulas have included the elementary "barbershop" phrase

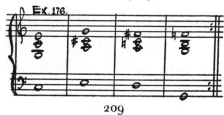

JAZZ: HOT AND HYBRID

repeated over and over again. In the hands of a capable "rhythm" section such formulas are, of course, considerably elaborated with rhythmic and pianistic embellishments and with typical jazz cadences.

Unlike the sophisticated jazz band, the hot ensemble seldom modulates from one key to another. Form, as a rule, is of the simplest cyclical variety, the basic harmonic phrase being repeated again and again with varying melodic and rhythmic contexts.

That most of the Negroid elements in Tin Pan Alley harmonization originated in hot playing of one sort or another is undoubtedly true. Today, however, there have been so many influences and counter influences in the harmonic field that it is impossible to guarantee the "primitiveness" of this element in conventional hot jazz music. All we can be sure of is that progressional harmony, a principle of purely European origin, has been influenced in a very peculiar manner by the American Negro, and that the influence has been felt to a greater or lesser extent in every variety of jazz.

Chapter 12

INFLUENCES FROM THE DARK CONTINENT

THE READER who has had the fortitude to follow the technical description of the preceding chapters will see that there is no simple answer to such questions as "Did the Negroes invent jazz?" and "Did the Negroes create the spirituals?" Over the latter question, in particular, much controversy has been and is still being waged, most of it on such superficial and comparatively irrelevant grounds as the similarity of texts and tunes as between White and allegedly Negroid products.

In the sense that jazz and the spirituals (as types of music) issued originally from Negro throats and Negro fingers, and would not have appeared at all except for the specific creative activity of the Negro, both arts are most assuredly Negroid.

When one examines the musical structure of these arts in detail, however, it becomes apparent that they represent a fusion of musical idioms in which both White and "African" contributions play indispensable roles. It is safe to say that virtually no Afro-American music today is wholly without White influence; and it is just as obvious that all jazz, from the most primitive hot variety to the most sophisticated, is heavily influenced by Negro musical habits.

Dividing all Afro-American music into the "hot" and "sophisticated" categories that we established at the beginning of the present discussion, it becomes obvious that the former division has provided the breeding ground for all the important "African" ingredients which have contributed to make jazz the individual and peculiar musical art that it is. Hot musical expression is the genuine art of the American Negro. Even hot expression is to a certain extent hybrid in nature. But it is purely Negroid in its peculiar aesthetic, in much of its melody and in virtually all of its rhythm. From it sophisticated musicians have drawn important ingredients of several more "Europeanized" forms of music—among them the concert spiritual and sweet jazz. These latter are less Negroid in aesthetic and in many points of technique, but an unmistakable Negroid flavor pervades them nevertheless.

In the preceding chapters we have taken apart and scrutinized the technical peculiarities that differentiate jazz from other types of music. With the possible exception of "barbershop" harmony, we have shown that all the differentiating elements are indisputably of Negro origin. We have seen that the dark-skinned inhabitants of the rural South embroidered their singing with polyrhythmic cycles, shifted melodic landmarks from strong to weak beats, chanted and spoke in the intonations of the blues scale, long before jazz was even heard of. We have seen how a great many of the more complex formulas of sophisticated commercial jazz writers are mere elaborations of conceptions that are fundamentally Negroid. We have seen how the European principle of progressional harmony, brought to the Negro in the early hymns and rural secular music of the Whites, was incorporated into his own religious expression; and how the intonations of his own speech and song affected in turn the progressions of this European structural principle. We have also seen how this principle has been similarly borrowed and similarly influenced by the Negro in forming the harmonic dialect of jazz.

Little reference to the actual music of the African continent has been made thus far. To establish the thesis that jazz is a Negroid product, it has been necessary merely to isolate its characteristic ingredients, demonstrate that they are foreign to White European musical usage, and trace them into the more primitive music and speech habits of the uneducated, rural Southern Negro.

Though much has been written by journalists about the jungle origins of jazz, proofs of any specific relationship between jazz and the music of Africa have been conspicuously lacking. In their accounts, musically untrained travelers and explorers have, as often as not, stressed the striking dissimilarity between African and American Negro music. Trained observers, like the late Henry Edward Krehbiel,[1] Natalie Curtis-Burlin,[2] and Nicholas G. J. Ballanta-Taylor,[3] have usually found some similarities to report. But their data, both as regards the structure of jazz and as regards the structure of native African music, have been too limited for a convincing demonstration.

Tracing jazz to Africa has proved a difficult business, primarily because so little is known, in relation to the territory involved, about the music of Africa. It is a very large continent, containing not only a vast field of distinct and dissimilar tribal customs, but considerable variation in racial character

[1] *Afro-American Folksongs,* G. Schirmer, New York, 1914.
[2] *Songs and Tales of the Dark Continent,* New York, 1908.
[3] Introduction to *St. Helena Island Spirituals,* Press of G. Schirmer, New York, 1925; and *Jazz Music in Its Relation to African Music,* in the *Musical Courier,* June 1922.

as well. Physical types, habits and music differ greatly as between one tribe and another. Coastal and North African regions which have been in contact, for centuries, with alien European, Semitic and Oriental peoples, often show the influences of these peoples in the local music. The Negro slaves of America's South, who arrived from widely separated African sources, must have brought with them a somewhat mixed musical heritage. It will take many more years of patient research by trained musical ethnologists before anything conclusive is known, even about the music of Africa itself. And only then will it be possible to say with any certainty, what part of the American Negro's music has a demonstrable African musical pedigree.[4]

Meanwhile however, certain odd scraps of verifiable information that are at hand, do tend to show that some germs of jazz are to be found in some varieties of African music. Among the most accessible reproductions of authentic African music at present are a set of phonographic recordings made by the Denis-Roosevelt African Expedition, and placed on sale a few years ago by the Reeves Sound Studios.[5] These records are engraved from the sound track of an extensive motion picture which was made with the assistance of the Belgian government.[6] They record singing, drumming and instrumental

---

[4] Though more than a thousand recordings of African tribal music are to be found in the archives of American libraries and museums, apparently no thorough, comprehensive musical analysis of their contents has as yet been undertaken. The largest collections include that of the Library of Congress, the Laura Bolton collection in Chicago, Melville J. Hershkovitz' collection at Northwestern University, George Herzog's collection at Columbia University, and collections at the University of Pennsylvania and at the New York Museum of Natural History.

[5] 1600 Broadway, New York City.

[6] Produced in American motion picture houses in a considerably edited version under the title *Dark Rapture*.

music of various tribes inhabiting the Belgian Congo and adjacent Tanganyika.

Immediately evident in these recordings is the polyphonic, syncopative character of the music's rhythm. Both the stimulating disruptiveness and the relentless continuity of jazz rhythm are represented here. But a more detailed inspection of the African rhythmic patterns reveals most of them to be based on fundamental pulses of triple rather than quadruple character. This is particularly noticeable in the fine recordings of the Royal Watusi drumming which occupy three sides of the Denis-Roosevelt discs. The Watusi drummers are amazingly resourceful and enthusiastic syncopators. But their fundamental rhythms are more like that of *The Campbells Are Coming* than like those of jazz. This same observation holds true for the rhythms of several other items in the series. In three or four, however, there is a basic rhythm of four, and some of these contain the three-over-four polyrhythmic superimposition characteristic of jazz rhythm. Perhaps the most striking example among them is that of the drumming which accompanies the Bapere Circumcision Ritual (Item 3 on the last side of the final disc.). Here two principal drums commence by establishing the fundamental pulse much as they might in the hands of a jazz drummer, or of a Cuban rumba percussionist:

Soon, however, they begin to break the unsyncopated monotony with a variation:

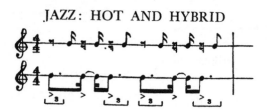

And the syncopated variation, heavily accented in the second drum, falls into the typical three-over-four polyrhythmic cycles. The resulting rhythm is strikingly like that of the rumba, and, of course, has its points of similarity to certain jazz constructions.

The following section of this disc, devoted to the interesting music of a Babira "stick orchestra," also contains the three-over-four rhythmic superimpositions, though the large spans of the fundamental rhythm are laid out in groups of three. The rhythm here (scalar elements omitted) is a bolero-type figure:

Sections of the Bapere drumming on side No. 3 also show traces of jazz polyrhythm. The complexity of the patterns, however, leaves some doubt as to whether the rhythm is really quadruple ($\frac{6}{4}$, i.e., $\frac{2}{4} + \frac{2}{4} + \frac{2}{4}$), or triple ($\frac{3}{16}$). It is also impossible to establish definitely which is the fundamental and which the superimposed rhythm:

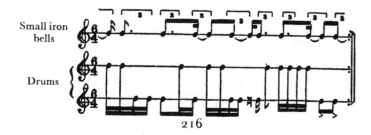

Small iron
bells

Drums

INFLUENCES FROM THE DARK CONTINENT

In the matter of scale and harmony, the Denis-Roosevelt recordings are somewhat less revealing, though here again there are traces of possible relationships to jazz. The blues scale, which we have found to be characteristic of so much American Negro music is lacking in the form in which it is used in America. There is frequent use of the flat seventh, however, and of the dominant seventh- and ninth-chord harmonies characteristic of blues harmonization. The pentatonic scale, as might be expected, is very prominent.

Except for the common "black-notes-of-the-piano" types of pentatonic, the most frequent scale in these recordings seems to be a curious five-tone series containing the tones of a Western dominant ninth-chord: [7]

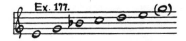

It does not seem to be characteristic of any one tribe, as it appears alike in the Babira songs (No. 2, second song), in the orchestral accompaniment to the *Dance of Chief Karumi* (No. 3, section 2), in all of the chanting, humming, flute-playing and drumming of the Mambuti Pigmies (Nos. 5 and 6), and in the chants of the Bapere Circumcision Ceremony (No. 12, section 1). In these various places it appears both as melody and as a monotonous one-chord harmony. In the Babira songs (where its harmonic use in the chord

[7] The presence of this scale in African music has been noted by Nicholas G. J. Ballanta-Taylor. See: *St. Helena Island Spirituals*, Foreword.

is particularly dwelt upon) it appears in the company of two simple pentatonic scales. There seem here to be four separate songs, the first and last of which are in the pentatonic scale:

Song No. 2 (sung after the change of key has been announced by the leader and duly confirmed by the chorus) employs a transposition of the ninth-chord series we have been considering:

Song No. 3 modulates to another pentatonic scale:

The sureness of intonation with which the primitive singers return to their original pentatonic scale for song No. 4 will interest those who like to speculate on the subject of absolute pitch.

An affection for the flat seventh is attested over and over again in these recordings. A particularly good example of this is found in the curious repetitious passages of pigmy flute music (No. 5, section 2):

To these observations the album of African records issued by Victor from the Laura Bolton collection [8] have comparatively little to add. The records chosen for this album have been made, in several cases, among peoples like the Tauregs and Swahilis whose music is strongly flavored with Oriental and Near Eastern ingredients. Polyrhythm appears in some of these, as it does extensively in the music of all North Africa, Arabia and India. It can scarcely be ascribed to Negro influence. Scalar structure is Semitic, and in some cases even European. In the more purely Negroid items there is a bewildering array of both scalar and rhythmic material which is too varied and scattered to draw conclusions from. Triple rhythm, like that in the Denis-Roosevelt Watusi drum records appears in Laura Bolton's Malinka *Song of Praise.* The Bakwiris and Binis evidently love to sing in parallel thirds almost as much as the Neapolitans and Mexicans do. A Malinka war song has a reiterated accompaniment on three drums (tuned approximately to the notes of a major triad) that strongly recalls the rumba rhythm:

[8] *African Music,* recorded by Laura C. Bolton on the Straus West African expedition of the Field Museum of Natural History.

JAZZ: HOT AND HYBRID

Where does all this point with reference to the ancestry of jazz? Only a few similarities are worth noting: First, though the blues scale is not indicated anywhere, the preference for one of its components—the flat seventh—is quite marked. Second, as in the case of the American Negro's music, the minor scale is slighted in favor of various major constructions. Third, the Africans show a genuine feeling for harmony (*i.e.*, chordic consonance), and in one of the Denis-Roosevelt songs (among the Mambetu songs on side No. 1) there is even evidence of a crude sort of harmonic progression from tonic to dominant and back again. Fourth, among the crude harmonic combinations used, one of the most prominent—the dominant seventh, or ninth-chord—points strikingly toward certain peculiarities of blues harmonization.

Chapter 13

THE JAZZ ORCHESTRA

THE ABSTRACT ELEMENTS of the jazz language that we have analyzed so far are characteristic of all jazz and of a great deal of other Afro-American music. They will be found in some proportion in the playing of any of our celebrated commercial "name" bands. They will also be found—in somewhat greater luxuriance—wherever a group of Southern Negroes manage to lay hands on a washboard, a harmonica, a kazoo and a couple of frying pans. The quality or interest of jazz depends on the instinctive musicianship of its players, not on the elaborateness or efficiency of the instruments it is played on. Nevertheless, jazz, in its professional forms, has been affected by what is known as jazz orchestration. And jazz orchestration has developed into a specialized technique, characteristically American and remarkably well-adapted, functionally, to the requirements of the jazz idiom. In the course of its development new instruments have been introduced into popular music, old instruments have found new and unsuspected fields of virtuosity, and a new principle of instrumental combination has been evolved.

The standard jazz band as we know it today is the product of an evolutionary, trial-and-error process that owes more to the popular entertainment industry and the ballroom than it does to the primitive jazz of the Southern Negroes. From the

221

point of view of instrumentation it is mainly a Northern and Western product. It contains several instruments—notably the saxophone and the piano—that were not characteristic of the bands of old New Orleans.[1] Its origins are more clearly traceable to the ragtime vaudeville and dance bands of the early 1900's, the Negro orchestras of Harlem, the hotel ball-room orchestras of the Pacific coast, the college and high-school dance orchestras of the first World War period.

On the whole, the history of jazz orchestration records a fairly consistent preference for certain instruments, which have been used in various combinations since the turn of the century. These are the piano, guitar, string bass, tuba, drums, clarinet, saxophone, trumpet, cornet and trombone. All of them are likely to be encountered in the modern band. Rarely in its history has jazz been played without some of them. The most consistently used of all are probably the trumpet, trombone, guitar (or banjo) and drums, which have been associated with practically all orchestral jazz from the early New Orleans period to the present.

The piano, today, ranks as the most important instrument used in jazz. It is the only one capable of giving a complete jazz performance unassisted, and jazz is practically never heard nowadays without it. Its ascendancy as an important solo constituent of the jazz band apparently dates from the late 1920's and 30's, when pianist band leaders like Duke Ellington and Fats Waller became prominent. But it was used, and even sometimes exploited, in ragtime bands of the 1890's. The celebrated Negro bandmaster Jim Reese Europe, who was active in Harlem and Carnegie Hall around 1912, was fond of using batteries of ten pianos at a time. The curious absence

[1] See Hobson: *American Jazz Music*, p. 98.

of pianos in the old New Orleans bands is probably accounted for by the fact that they often performed in parades and on wagons where pianos were awkward to handle. In the brothels of the old Storyville section of New Orleans, jazz and ragtime piano playing was, of course, a commonplace long before the turn of the century. It was this sort of piano playing that the White pianist Ben Harney brought North in the 1890's to the astonishment and delight of patrons at Tony Pastor's. The entire ragtime era, as we have seen earlier, was dominated by the piano.

The saxophone's career is a remarkably checkered one considering its reputation as the jazz instrument *par excellence*. As we have noted above, it was almost never used in early Southern jazz; and it has tended definitely to fall out of fashion with jazz connoisseurs since the "swing" craze of the 1930's. It rose to overwhelming prominence in the bands of the 1920's, where its somewhat mawkish, almost human tone quality fitted the sweet song-style jazz popular with Paul Whiteman and his followers. It has always been associated with large bands rather than small combinations. And it has always been a mainstay of commercial "sweet" jazz. There have, of course, been a number of famous hot saxophone players, and large hot bands like Fletcher Henderson's and Duke Ellington's have always employed saxophones. But because of its tone, its showy appearance and its usefulness for lush, sentimental effects, it is apt to suggest the polite dance floor or the movie-house spotlight type of jazz rather than the hot variety. The first bandleader to make regular use of batteries of three or four saxophones was probably Art Hickman of San Francisco's St. Frances Hotel orchestra. Hickman's example, which dates from around 1914, has since been emulated by every subsequent "sweet" dance-band leader.

The saxophone was by no means new when the dance bands of the first World War period began adopting it. It was a familiar instrument in popular outdoor music long before that time. This particular phase of its history has, for some reason, been overlooked by most writers, and the impression has been given that the saxophone was rescued by jazz artists from a comparative oblivion into which it had fallen since its occasional use by such French operatic composers as Meyerbeer and Ambroise Thomas. As a matter of fact the saxophone held a place as one of the most important and valued instruments of the military band all through the later decades of the past century. Invented by the famous Parisian instrument maker, Antoine Joseph Adolphe Sax, about 1840, it was almost immediately adopted as an indispensable constituent of the French army bands, and its popularity subsequently spread to other nations. Though the English and Americans seem to have taken it up somewhat later than the continental Europeans, its position was solidly established in our brass-band instrumentation in the 'seventies and 'eighties. In the post-Civil War years the most famous concert band in America was that of the redoubtable Irish bandmaster Patrick Sarsfield Gilmore. Pictures dating from 1875 show "Pat" Gilmore's band appearing in Madison Square Garden with a full quartet of saxophones. Since military bands often did duty at large balls and dances at this period, even converting military marches into two-steps, there was plenty of precedent for using the saxophone as a dance-hall instrument long before the jazz players adopted it.

The tenor banjo offers another case of the supposedly typical

THE JAZZ ORCHESTRA

jazz instrument whose reputation is not backed up by consistent use. Musicologists are generally agreed that it is a genuine African contribution to instrumentation, and it was always the characteristic instrument of the old minstrel shows. Early Southern jazz bands sometimes employed it, but were just as apt to employ the more resourceful guitar in its place. The big commercial bands of the 1920's used it, partly for its strong, twanging contribution to the rhythm section, but partly too, because it looked appropriate and was regarded as a sort of trade mark of jazz during that period. Since then it has tended to disappear almost entirely. Today, it still has a few faithful adherents, but in the vast majority of bands it has been replaced by the guitar.

The earliest standardized form of the jazz orchestra seems to be the New Orleans band of 1900. There is, of course, no record of it on phonograph discs. Present-day devotees of what they fondly call the "New Orleans style" would probably be somewhat disconcerted by the sound of the music it actually produced. It is certain that it resembled the smooth, hot, supposed New Orleans revivals of the 1920's very little. Our only indisputable clues today to the actual character of old New Orleans jazz are the rather rough, foursquare brass-band-like recordings made by the famous Original Dixieland Band in 1918. And the Dixieland Band, though from New Orleans, was neither a Negro, nor a typical New Orleans, band. It consisted of a trumpet, a clarinet, a piano and drums.

The typical New Orleans bands, which apparently originated with Buddy Bolden's in the late 1890's, must have produced a rather raw, brassy and harmonically thin type of music. They consisted as a rule of a trumpet, a trombone, a clarinet, a string bass, drums and a banjo or guitar. In Buddy Bolden's band

225

the trombone was not a slide but a valve instrument, which meant that the "sliphorn" techniques of later jazz were absent. A violin was often added to this combination, perhaps mainly as a gesture toward musical gentility. The whole effect must have been rather primly primitive compared to the smooth technical dexterity of later jazz. It is not impossible that it sounded somewhat like the jerky music of the contemporary piano rag. When the New Orleans bands moved North with the breakup of the old Storyville red light district around 1918, the classical simplicity of this combination was quickly lost. "King" Oliver, one of the first bandleaders to settle permanently in Chicago, added a piano to his band in the process, thereby inaugurating a small-scale instrumentation that was to become typical of Chicago, rather than New Orleans jazz. The special New Orleans jazz tradition undoubtedly contributed much to the development of jazz as a popular art form, but its contributions in the field of orchestration were soon to be superseded.

Much present writing by the *aficionados* of the "New Orleans style" gives the impression that the North, East and West knew practically nothing of jazz until the New Orleans Negroes brought the art to Chicago. This, of course, is misleading. By the time "King" Oliver and his associates went to work seriously in Chicago, the country had already been teeming with jazz bands from coast to coast for nearly a decade. Many of the old New Orleans bands had toured widely on vaudeville circuits. Hot jazz was already a familiar thing in Harlem and New York's famous Roseland ballroom. Sweet jazz, for dancing purposes, was a commonplace in high schools and colleges. Sweet jazz pioneers like Art Hickman of San Francisco's St. Francis Hotel, had been playing jazz, of a smooth, melodious sort, since 1914. Paul Whiteman was about to organize the first of his big jazz bands, and was shortly to appear at the Palais Royal in New York. For nearly fifteen years, jazz in one form or another had made sporadic appearances in the larger American cities. It was not called jazz at the time, but it was a different sort of music from that played by old-fashioned restaurant and hotel orchestras. It employed saxophones and characteristic rhythm sections as early as 1905, when Will Marion Cook's Memphis Students appeared for a stand at Proctor's Twenty-third Street Theatre in New York. It may have been indifferent jazz, some of it encumbered with vaudeville clowning, some of it mawkishly sentimental. But it all spoke a new syncopated musical language. And by the end of the first World War it was becoming a fairly standardized art form, and assuming the character of a popular musical revolution.

Perhaps 1917 marked as nearly as any other year the development of this revolution on a national scale. The picture of American popular music at the time was a confusing one, and its outlines did not really clarify until later. Theatre and movie-house orchestras suddenly began to change their orchestration following the new style introduced by the hotel dance bands. Tin Pan Alley arrangers began introducing saxophones into their standard commercial orchestrations and leaving out instruments like second violins, oboes and cellos. Three years later the song hit *Whispering* was to be moaned incessantly from the maws of saxophones in every hamlet in the country. Ragtime piano playing, alone, or combined with drums, violins, trumpets, trombones and so forth, had been going great guns all over America since 1900, and with special exuberance since 1910. The large jazz band, as a standardized orchestral combination, was now succeeding the ragtime combination, and was already pretty well set in its orchestration. The New Orleans Negro musicians like Louis Armstrong and "King" Oliver, who came North at this time, perhaps found the Northern tradition of instrumentation an improvement on the New Orleans variety. Or perhaps the immense popularity of the larger Northern bands bowled them over. At any rate, they practically all joined or formed Northern type bands in Chicago, and nobody ever heard a real old-style New Orleans band again.

This Northern and Western type of band, which was to become the standard jazz orchestra of the twenties and remains standard even today, ranged in size from eight to fifteen men. The latter number was rarely exceeded. At full strength it consisted of three "units," a division recognized by all jazz orchestras of the period. These were the brass unit, the reed unit and the rhythm unit. The brass unit commonly comprised two to three trumpets and two to three trombones; the reeds, two to four (usually four) saxophones and a clarinet (sometimes played as an alternate instrument by one of the saxophonists); the rhythm unit, a piano, a guitar (or banjo), a bass tuba (or string bass) and a set of drums. This was the type of orchestra used (with occasional amplifications) by virtually all the big name bands from Whiteman to Glenn Miller and from Fletcher Henderson to Duke Ellington. There were also smaller varieties. The standard orchestrations of the Tin Pan Alley publishers were aimed for years at a somewhat more modest ten-man combination distributed as follows: two trumpets and a trombone; three saxophones; piano, tenor banjo, tuba or string bass, drums; solo violin. Curiously the solo violin clung as tenaciously to the standard bands of the

THE JAZZ ORCHESTRA

1920's as it had to the old New Orleans bands, I suspect partly because the leaders of many theatre orchestras of the period were violinists and had to be considered by the Tin Pan Alley orchestrators. As a jazz instrument, the violin has never been much of a success except in the hands of a few isolated specialists like the very gifted jazz fiddler Joe Venuti. Still smaller combinations were frequently found among the improvising bands. The commonest of these were perhaps the eight- and ten-man bands comprising one or two trumpets, a trombone, a clarinet, one or two saxophones, piano, guitar, bass and drums.

A few things are worth noting about the distribution of instruments in these combinations. First, the brass, reeds and rhythm units were in each case fairly evenly represented. Second, there was always a piano. Third, saxophones were practically always present, and in the larger combinations were used in powerful batteries of three and four at a time. The four rhythm instruments (piano, guitar, bass and drums) apparently enjoyed an indispensable standing not granted to the other units. When the size of the orchestra was reduced, it was brass or reeds that were eliminated. Evidently four rhythm men were required whether the band was an eight- or a fifteen-man outfit.

The system of "units" was somewhat analogous to the classical division of the symphony orchestra into "choirs" of strings, woodwinds, brass and percussion. And, in miniature, the units were often handled by jazz arrangers as a classical composer handles symphonic choirs. But units of saxophones, brass and percussion were really evolved for a different function from that of their symphonic counterparts. This function had to do with the internal structure of jazz. As has been remarked

229

previously, the constitution of the standard jazz ensemble was probably strongly influenced by the harmonic, melodic and rhythmic character of the song-style jazz that followed the vogue of the blues. This musical genre, and the jazz that grew out of it, demanded instruments capable of imitating the emotional inflections of Negro declamation. As a melodic instrument the violin, for example, was by nature too restrained and formal. Its range, too, was in general somewhat high for this sort of declamatory utterance. And it was a difficult instrument, played generally by cultivated, literate musicians who did not have the capacity for abandon, or the Afro-American rhythmic sense, that jazz required. The flute, for another example, was too unemotional an instrument, too limited in its range of dynamic contrasts.

It is important also in this connection to remember the differences in musical texture between the popular idiom of Europe, for which the old-fashioned café or theatre orchestra was designed, and the new jazz idiom. The European style theatre orchestra, with its fairly complete choirs of strings, woodwind and brass, answered to the demands of a type of music whose structure was to some extent contrapuntal. The music of the Viennese and the Parisian operetta, and the Anglo-Celtic music-hall and folk tradition often echoed, however simply, the polyphonic niceties of the more complex forms of European composition. Jazz, on the other hand, is not a contrapuntal type of music—not, at any rate, in the sense that the term applies to European music. It seldom employed the conventional four-voiced harmonic structure that is the basis of classical European composition. The new Negroid idiom involved no "inner voices" or complex melodic basses. It consisted basically of a sustained melody moving over a throbbing rhythmic background, with just enough harmonic material thrown in to define a simple sequence of chords.

Hence, the polyphonic balance provided for by the old-fashioned popular ensemble became obsolete for jazz players. The new idiom required a few melodic instruments of dynamically flexible quality, and a sturdy array of accompanying rhythm-makers. The trumpet, trombone, clarinet and saxophone supplied the former category; the piano, guitar, string bass and drums the latter. Melodic counterpoint—what there was of it—was limited to upper voices. The piano and guitar added all that was needed in the way of harmony.

The commercial jazz orchestrators of the twenties, largely under Whiteman's influence, attempted for a time to convert the jazz band into an orchestral variety show. In doing so, they overloaded the jazz idiom with so many foreign sophisticated ingredients that the result hardly resembled jazz at all. This was the era of "symphonic" jazz, of *Whispering* and *Song of India*, of batteries of shining brass instruments that took the auditor's breath away with their sheer visual luxuriance before he had had a chance to listen to the music. "Auxiliary" instruments without number were added to the band. The celesta, with its sentimental tinkling chords, became almost a standard instrument in the larger bands. So did the oboe, which, as a contemporary arranger, Arthur Lange,[2] sagaciously remarked, was "useful for Oriental effects." Orchestral bells, xylophones, vibraphones, vibraharps, piano accordions, Hawaiian steel guitars, even bassoons, flutes and French horns added to the variety of jazz orchestration. Some bands even had fairly complete string choirs. The jazz arranger began to assume the

[2] Lange, Arthur, *Arranging for the Modern Dance Orchestra*, Robbins Music Corporation, New York, 1926.

position of paramount importance which he still retains in the field of commercial, sweet jazz. He was technically proficient and resourceful. He still is. It is largely his ingenuity in creating instrumental, melodic and harmonic variations, in introducing apt modulations, in evolving slick and striking orchestral textures, that makes Tin Pan Alley's and Hollywood's tunes wear as well as they do. His proficiency was seconded by a remarkable development in instrumental technique among the sweet jazz artists. Saxophones, clarinets, trumpets and trombones were made to do things they had never done in the hands of European-style symphonic musicians.

But all this had, essentially, very little to do with jazz. And the big variety-show type of jazz band's power to astound was limited to audiences of musical yokels who had never experienced the infinitely greater resources of the symphony orchestra. It is not surprising that "symphonic" jazz shortly fell from fashion. Its regimental proportions and carefully rehearsed arrangements killed any impulse its players may have had toward free flights of improvisation. As jazz it was dead and embalmed. To the sensitive music lover, its plushy tone and pat, gilded, exotic, orchestral effects were always the very essence of musical vulgarity. "Symphonic" jazz came to represent in American music about what Grauman's Chinese Theatre in Hollywood or Roxy's theatre in New York represent in American architecture. It achieved the perfect fusion of the pretentious and the commonplace that defines bad taste.

Meanwhile, in less fashionable and theatrical surroundings, good jazz continued to be played. Much of it was played by small combinations, but much was also played by large bands of the standardized type described earlier in this chapter. Practically all the leading hot players of the twenties did excellent improvisatory work with combinations of from ten to fifteen players. Most of what is highly praised today as "New Orleans style" was recorded in Chicago and New York during the 1920's; and virtually none of it was played with the original New Orleans type of instrumentation.

Small combinations built around a piano remained popular with jazz *aficionados*, however, throughout the Chicago period. Later, in 1935, with the rise of the "swing" craze their popularity increased all over the country. Unlike the large bands, these small combinations were not standardized except in the rhythm section, which usually consisted of the inevitable piano, guitar, string bass and drums. To these were added, variously, a trumpet and a couple of saxophones; or a trumpet, trombone, clarinet and saxophone; or two trumpets and two saxophones, and so on. Then there were the still smaller combinations—trios, quartets, sextets, etc.—which performed some of the most delicate and freely improvised jazz that has ever been heard. Some of the best of these have been very eccentric in instrumentation. The Adrian Rhythmic Trio consisted of a vibraphone, a guitar and a string bass; the famous Hot Club of France Quintet, of three guitars, a violin and a string bass.

The standardized art of jazz orchestration, however, is not really represented in these smaller groups. Jazz can be played with the simplest and most eccentric of instrumental combinations. And often the simpler the combination is, the better the jazz sounds. It is the purpose of this chapter simply to record the fact that a new type of orchestration accompanied the growth of jazz as a popular musical phenomenon and became standardized in the layout of the large jazz band. The importance of this development to the art of jazz is debatable.

The instrumentation of jazz is not its most vital aspect. But, for better or for worse, the America of the post-World-War-I period begot the jazz band. And it has since become our most characteristic vehicle for the performance of popular music.

Chapter 14

AESTHETICS AND THE MUSICAL
FORM OF JAZZ

IT HAS LONG been customary to discuss those aspects of music
that are measured in terms of time under two headings. The
shorter time-patterns—those involving single notes or small
groups of notes—are commonly referred to under "rhythm,"
while the temporal relationships between larger spans—
phrases, themes, movements and so on—fall into the category
of "musical form." The distinction between the two headings
is not always altogether precise. "Rhythm" and "musical
form" often deal respectively with shorter or more extended
manifestations of very similar phenomena. And cases sometimes present themselves that are just as readily classified under
one as under the other.

In hot jazz, as in other types of music, "musical form" has
certain relationships to "rhythm"; and just as its rhythmic
structure differs in some respects from European rhythmic
structure, so its "musical form" differs in certain respects from
European "musical form." And it is not surprising to find that
the differences in "form" between jazz and European music
parallel in various ways the differences in "rhythm."

We have seen how the Negro employs syncopation of
various sorts (including polyrhythm, melodic displacement and
so on) as a basic structural principle. This structural principle

applies not only to small rhythmic patterns, but often exerts an influence over the formation of large phrases, and thus invades the field ordinarily discussed under "form." Some of its manifestations in this field are quite foreign to the European habit of musical thought, involving, indeed, a wholly different approach to the art from that of the European musician. This aspect of jazz, which incidentally has a great deal to do with the fundamental character of jazz rhythm, unfortunately cannot be illustrated by parallel examples showing differences between Negroid and European usage. The difference here is a difference not only of technical structure, but of aesthetic function. Our approach to this problem must start, at least, in the psychological sphere.

Syncopation, even in its simplest forms, has certain definite effects upon the nervous system. The precise nature and extent of these effects would provide a large and interesting field for some laboratory psychologist to exploit. We need not trouble ourselves here in speculating about details that research workers will no doubt someday track down. Sufficient to our present purposes to note that these effects do exist as a matter of demonstrable, every-day experience. The interruption of rhythmic regularity produces a feeling of unrest. The listener's rhythmic faculties are thrown off balance, and he gropes instinctively for a re-orientation. His groping is attended by a certain sense of stimulation or excitement. A resumption of regularity is greeted with a feeling of relief.

In this psychological phenomenon we have the basis of a structural principle. Unrest followed by relief, in one form or another, is fundamental to a great deal of art. It has been an essential element of narration from the Greek drama to the detective story. It is found in music in many forms. The "da capo" principle, involving the return of a familiar theme following a passage of unfamiliar material, is a manifestation of it. Symphonic form, with its "recapitulation" of original themes following an adventurous "development section," is another and more elaborate one. The tendency to end a composition in its original key, despite intervening modulations that have led far afield, is still another illustration of this formal axiom. Its most obvious manifestation in European music is, perhaps, in the principle of consonance and dissonance. A discord produces a feeling of unrest and demands "resolution" to a concord which relieves that feeling. All of these musical manifestations of the unrest-relief aesthetic concept involve, however, fields of harmony, melody, key-relationship and so on. The production of similar psychological results by purely rhythmic means—as in syncopation—is only rarely found in European music, and then only as a device involving short patterns of sequence. In other words, syncopation in Western music is an occasionally employed device belonging to the category of "rhythm." Seldom if ever does it invade the category of "musical form."

Now, in jazz—and in a great deal of the music of the Orient —the production of unrest and relief by purely rhythmic means is a fundamental principle of musical structure. Not only does syncopation occupy an analogous position here to that occupied by consonance and dissonance in Western music; but the syncopative principle here becomes so elaborated that it invades the field of "musical form" as well as that of "rhythm." The syncopation in these types of music is not only a note-against-note phenomenon, but may involve the distortion of phraseological as well as "rhythmic" regularity.

Perhaps the simplest example of this phenomenon in jazz is

provided by the "break." This device, which entered commercial jazz with the "blues" influence, consists of a sort of bridge-passage that is tacked on to the end of a melodic phrase, filling out the dead interval that elapses between the final cadence of this phrase and the beginning of the following phrase. "Breaks" are seldom more than two or four measures in length. In sophisticated jazz they are usually played by a single solo instrument while the rest of the orchestra remains silent. In less sophisticated Negroid music—particularly in "blues"—they often fill up the long intervals between vocal phrases where the singer pauses for breath. The Bessie Smith recordings of *You've Been a Good Ole Wagon* and the *St. Louis* and *Cold in Hand Blues*, contain very interesting piano and cornet breaks.

The break occupies a position in jazz that is not altogether unlike that of the cadenza in classical bravura music. As was originally the case with the cadenza, the break, even in sophisticated jazz, is usually improvised. The jazz composer and orchestrator do not write it out. It is left to the ingenuity, imagination, and momentary impulse of the solo performer. Like the cadenza, it appears at the close of a more substantial and regular musical statement, and immediately precedes a resumption of the logical pattern of sequence. Where the cadenza elaborates the "restless" dominant harmony, delaying its resolution to the "reposeful" final tonic chord by a lengthened fioritura passage, the break involves a "restless" series of unaccompanied syncopations which "resolve" with a "reposeful" resumption of the accompaniment.

The break, then, is a temporary lapse from the rigors of strict structure, in which logic is momentarily suspended and improvisatory chaos reigns. Its effect is to heighten the element of suspense and unrest. The listener is thrown for the moment on unmapped and confusing ground. The basic rhythm ceases to offer its familiar thumping landmarks. The solo dangles dizzyingly without support, and then, just as the listener has about abandoned hope of re-orienting himself, the fundamental rhythm resumes its orderly sway, and a feeling of relief ensues.

In this process the fundamental rhythm is not really destroyed. The perceptive listener holds in his mind a continuation of its regular pulse even though the orchestra has stopped marking it. And when the orchestra resumes its rhythmic function, it continues the series of mentally sustained pulses, its entrance coinciding precisely with one of them. The situation during the silent pulses is one that challenges the listener to hold his bearings. If he has any sort of rhythmic sense he will not be content to lose himself. If he does not feel the challenge, or is perfectly content to lose himself, then he is one of those who will never understand the appeal of jazz. The challenge is backed up by the chaotic behavior of the solo instrument playing the break. It does everything possible to throw the listener off his guard. It syncopates; it accents everything *but* the normal pulse of the fundamental rhythm; it attempts to distract the listener in every conceivable manner from the series of regular pulses he is attempting to hold in his mind. The listener feels all the exhilaration of battle. Often, of course, he exhibits physical symptoms, stamping his feet or bobbing his head in order to maintain his sense of orientation. The power of such devices over the motor impulses is notorious.

It is not often that the musician or the really acute listener loses sight of the fundamental rhythm, in spite of the influence of the break rhythms. What actually happens is that the mind perceives, and maintains contact with, two simultaneous and conflicting channels of rhythm, one of which is heard, the other sustained in the imagination.

This phenomenon of simultaneous rhythms, playing against each other, is, of course, not limited to the break. We have already discussed it in connection with the smaller patterns of rhythm in our chapter on "hot rhythm." The break merely represents the principle of syncopation operating on somewhat larger spans of musical structure. In hot improvisation the entire flow of musical form is likely to exhibit the same phenomenon. Indeed, certain types of hot jazz may practically be said to consist of an indefinite series of breaks.

In this connection let us consider that minor, specialized form of jazz known as tap dancing. It offers an admirable example here because it is purely percussive, and therefore relatively simple. The tap dancer is commonly accompanied in what is known as "stop time." The orchestra, or instruments, accompanying him play, softly, the bare skeleton of a jazz tune. The skeleton consists of a series of short, clipped chords marking the main melodic features of the tune, and coinciding as a rule, with pulses of the fundamental rhythm. Rarely does "stop time" involve a syncopation; only, in fact, when the syncopation is so characteristic a feature of the original melody that it cannot be eliminated. The tunes used for the purpose are usually slow ones that offer relatively few melodic complexities per phrase, and their "stop time" versions often contain an average of only one or two chords, or notes, per measure.

Upon this skeletonized framework the tap dancer embroiders a rhythmic improvisation. The chords of the "stop

AESTHETICS AND THE MUSICAL FORM OF JAZZ

time" accompaniment provide him with points of reference;
in other words with a widely spaced series of pulses representing the fundamental rhythm. His own improvisation plays
against this rhythm, filling up the intervals between the "stop
time" chords with percussive patterns and polyrhythmic cycles
that answer to different systems of accent from that represented by the fundamental rhythm. As in the case of the
"break," the tap dancer's phrase represents a take-off into
rhythmic abandon, and a subsequent return to the normality
of the fundamental rhythm. Here, also, a play of two conflicting rhythms is involved. Each time interval between the
chords of the "stop time" accompaniment constitutes a small
percussive "break." The listener's sense of rhythmic orientation is disturbed by the syncopation of the dancer's feet. He
fights the sense of unrest that this phenomenon induces, and
then he is relieved by the appearance of the faithful fundamental pulse which appears just where he expected, or hoped,
to find it.

In hot jazz the musical resources—melody, timbre, harmony
—are richer. But the principle of construction is the same. It
is the battle between the unexpected, restless, challenging
rhythm of hot melody and the regularity of the fundamental
pulse that is to blame for the particular sense of exhilaration
known popularly as "swing." The full sense of swing is, naturally, seldom felt except in purely improvisatory jazz. When
even the players themselves are not quite sure what is going
to happen next the music takes on the aspect of a tussle in
which individual players may actually try to unhorse each
other, as well as the audience, by means of conflicting rhythmic
impacts. When players, dancers and audience alike are hang-
ing desperately to their sense of rhythmic orientation on one

hand and are violently disturbing it (or listening to it being violently disturbed) on the other, the result is jazz in its purest form.

This aesthetic principle is, however, neither new nor peculiar to jazz. On the same basis of structure the Hindus have built an elaborate and subtle musical art, whose rhythms are infinitely more complex than any so far dreamed of in jazz. It is interesting and instructive to compare the two arts because of the light such a comparison throws on those aspects of jazz that have little or no relation to Western music. That there has been some intermingling of the idioms of India and the Moslem peoples of the Near East with those of the African Negro is not improbable. That the rhythmic structure of jazz is a derivative from these sources would be difficult to prove, however. More likely is it that the Negro, being an improviser and a sensitive rhythmist, evolved, independently of the Southern Asiatics, a type of music that rests on similar structural principles. In any case jazz in its purely rhythmic aspects is much more primitive and much more limited, than the art music of Southern Asia.

If we examine the type of music known in North India as *gath*—and it is, I believe, a music of Mohammedan origin— we will find a remarkable flowering of the structural principle we have just been describing.[1] Here there is a "fundamental rhythm" whose pulses are always kept in mind by the player, though they may only be marked in the music itself at wide intervals. This "fundamental rhythm," moreover, is not necessarily limited to four-quarter or two-quarter time as is the case in jazz, but may be measured in several different meters. On

[1] See Winthrop Sargeant and Sarat Lahiri: *A Study in East Indian Rhythm,* Musical Quarterly, October 1931.

this basic framework an instrumentalist—say, a *vina* [2] player —improvises a type of composition that partakes of the elements of both our "rondo" and our "variation" forms. His improvisation contains at least one melodic phrase, or group of notes, which tends to recur again and again, serving as a sort of melodic landmark and providing a unifying element of familiarity. This little phrase invariably appears on a beat of the fundamental rhythm and is the listener's and player's guarantee against chaos. Between its appearances the music is of "break" character. The instrumentalist syncopates in very subtle and complicated ways, and his "breaks" are often what we would call measures and measures in length—long enough to make even the average Western musician with a "good sense of rhythm" lose all track of fundamental bearings. It is interesting to note that polyrhythm forms a very important part of his technique. It is not, however, limited to three-over-four superimpositions (though these are popular). Superimpositions for the East Indian musician are virtually unlimited in variety. Seven over four, five over three, ten over two—cycles involving practically every number of rhythmic units are quite common. The rhythmic sense that permits the musician to keep a continuous and changing chain of such cycles perfectly oriented with regard to the fundamental pulse (which here is not stated musically as in jazz, but is merely borne in mind) involves something on the order of mathematical genius. On the rhythmic side this sort of music is to jazz what integral calculus is to elementary arithmetic.

Moreover the syncopating instrumentalist is usually accompanied by a drummer who is studiously occupied in creating

[2] A large guitar-like stringed instrument used by the finest Hindu musicians.

an altogether different chain of complex "breaks" built on the same fundamental rhythm, but involving syncopations and polyrhythmic cycles that play against those of the melody. At stated intervals the two players join each other in a return to the fundamental pulse. And each time they deviate again, often testing their syncopatory skill by attempting to destroy each other's sense of the fundamental pulse while retaining their own. The East Indian *gath* is constructed in terms of not two, but three simultaneous and conflicting streams of rhythm, one of which (the fundamental rhythm) is not explicitly stated but merely held in the mind.

This sort of musical structure is, of course, only possible in an improvisatory art. Surprise and suspense are integral to the aesthetic scheme of the East Indian *gath*. Rehearsal or "interpretation" from written notes would immediately spoil it by introducing the foreign element of deliberateness. The Hindu musician possesses a system of notation by means of which he can write his music down, but he seldom employs it. Why, indeed, should he deliberately reduce to cold, meaningless symbols a type of art whose essence cannot be expressed by them? As to preserving his creations for posterity: why should he? Posterity will make its own *gaths*. And anyway he wouldn't want anybody imitating his own particular style of *gath* creation, supposing anyone was as unimaginative as to want to imitate instead of creating himself. Furthermore, the Hindu *ustad*, or master musician, never plays a *gath* twice in exactly the same way. He would consider the suggestion that he do so as an insult to his powers of imagination. His music must be "hot," or it is nothing.

Superficially, of course, there is little resemblance between hot jazz and the music of India. The former has elements of harmony that are foreign to the latter. The former is also much more limited in the matter of scale, as well as in rhythm. But in psychological effect, and in essential qualities of rhythmic structure, there are certain resemblances between the two. And in these peculiarities jazz invades a dimension totally foreign to the music of the West.

*   *   *   *   *

Thus there is a somewhat closer relationship between the various sections of a jazz improvisation than is indicated by the simple formula of its phraseological structure. In actual performance there is a dynamic quality which arises from the "unrest-relief" principle described above—and this leads from phrase to phrase, giving a certain element of suspense to what is, coldly considered, a very simple type of "variation" form.

Considered as we consider "musical form" in Western music, jazz has a rather elementary structure. The hot ensemble simply presents a theme, which may be improvised or taken from some popular melody, and proceeds to make a series of rhythmic and melodic variations on it. The harmonic structure of the theme is not altered in the variations. The formula is that usually expressed in theory books as $A + A' + A'' + A'''$ etc.; in other words the simple theme-and-variation type of structure.

Within the scheme of this formula there are several common variants. Popular Tin Pan Alley songs usually consist of a "verse," or introductory stanza, and a "chorus," which constitutes the main melody. The phraseological structure of these component parts usually answers to common European principles of song form. In semi-improvisatory jazz performance the "chorus," and variations upon it, usually appear more frequently than the "verse" and its variations. There seems to be no precise rule as to which precedes or follows which. The "verse" may even be omitted altogether, and the "chorus" alone used as the theme for the variations. Phraseological structure is usually in units of four, eight or sixteen measures, except in "blues" which are usually laid out in phrases of twelve measures. There are, of course, exceptional forms to be found in more sophisticated hot playing. Some of these are of "fantasy" or "rhapsody" character. They are not common however. It is notable in this connection that the hot ensemble usually sticks to a single key throughout an entire improvisation. It seldom modulates.

The sweet jazz arranger has, of course, developed his more deliberate and more elaborate recipes for giving a jazz tune extended form. These need hardly concern us at length here. Again the process is one of variation form, the completed orchestral version being known, in the language of the craft, as a "routine." A typical routine is laid out as follows: [3]

Introduction (A short phrase in the key of the composition).
(B)   Verse (In the original key).
(A)   First Chorus (In the original key with slight change in orchestration).
(A')   Second Chorus (In the original key with altogether different orchestration).
(A")   Third Chorus (In a higher key).
          (This is sometimes known as the "Arranger's Chorus" because of the fact that here the greatest

[3] See Lange, Arthur, *Arranging for the Modern Dance Orchestra*, New York, 1926.

AESTHETICS AND THE MUSICAL FORM OF JAZZ

> liberties of orchestration and rhythmic variation
> occur.)
(A)   Fourth or Final Chorus (In the original key).

There are, of course, many types of routine, some affected by individual arrangers, others more or less standard.

The lack of complexity or variety in the conventional formal layout of hot jazz is due primarily to the lack of any creative development in the harmonic dimension of jazz. Jazz harmony, as we have previously seen (Chapter 11) is highly standardized, quite unimaginative, very simple and not subject to the improvisatory variation that gives the melodic and rhythmic features of jazz continued interest. Jazz has this feature of harmonic monotony in common with most folk music, which in this respect is sharply differentiated from the harmonically inventive art of concert music. Claims have sometimes been made by writers that hot jazz musicians improvise "counterpoint," and it is true that melodies are improvised simultaneously in most hot jazz. But the use of the word "counterpoint" in this connection is really based on a misapprehension. The simultaneous melodies of hot jazz are not fitted together neatly according to the laws of a highly perfected intellectual technique such as the one that produces canons and fugues. Their coordination is to a large extent accidental, and occurs mainly because the harmonic framework on which they are based is so simple that nearly anything played with reference to it is bound to "go together." Any careful harmonic analysis of these "contrapuntal" hot jazz passages will reveal, underneath the apparent freedom of improvised melody, a sturdy repetition of one of a half dozen simple, monotonous chord sequences.

Jazz has, however, made one contribution in the field of

conventional musical form: the peculiar twelve-bar stanza characteristic of the blues and of boogie woogie piano playing. This form, if it ever existed in European or white American folk music, has certainly been rather exceptional there. Yet it is a remarkably satisfying and "natural" sounding kind of musical structure, eminently suited to the slow songs of lamentation which developed in connection with it. The novelty in blues form (aside from its harmonic peculiarities which we considered earlier) is basically a matter of musical prosody, which here falls into stanzas of three, instead of the conventional two or four lines. This stanza form is apparent in the words of most blues songs, which fall naturally into this sort of triplet verse. Often the first two lines are identical. There are countless examples. A very primitive one, quoted in Helen L. Kaufmann's *From Jehovah to Jazz*, goes:

> *Gwine take morphine an' die,*
> *Gwine take morphine an' die,*
> *Gwine take morphine an' die.*

The following two, slightly more pretentious, samples come from John and Alan Lomax's *American Ballads and Folksongs:*

> *Well-a Shorty George, he ain' no friend of mine,*
> *Well-a Shorty George, he ain' no friend of mine,*
> *Taken all de womens an' leave de mens behin'.*

> *I's tired of livin', pretty mama, I don' know what to do.*
> *I's tired of livin', pretty mama, I don' know what to do.*
> *You is tired of me, babe, an I is tired of you.*

Musically this form produces the twelve-bar blues phrase

(*i.e.*, three small phrases of 4 bars each) which has been taken over by the boogie woogie pianists as the basis of a variation form. The busily thumping bass that the boogie woogie pianist plays with his left hand is usually a rhythmic elaboration of the blues chord sequence notated on p. 166. It is played over and over again without the slightest variation. Meanwhile, the right hand is free to do with melodies, runs and chords what the blues singer does with his voice. It improvises variations in the blues scale, elaborating on the steady harmonic framework provided by the bass. Apart from its peculiar twelve-bar phraseology, boogie woogie is closely related to the classical *chaconne* and *passacaglia*, the former of which is a variation form based on a continuously repeated sequence of chords, the latter a somewhat similar form based on a continuously repeated melodic bass phrase.

The formal layout of jazz phrases and routines is thus a fairly simple matter compared with the corresponding structure of concert music. But, as we have seen earlier in this chapter, the "form" of jazz is not wholly explicable in terms of cut-and-dried formula. Some of its more characteristic aspects invade a musical dimension that is quite alien to Western musical culture. This dimension, long familiar to the Southern Asiatics and North Africans, is peculiar to improvised music. To compare the phraseological structure of jazz with that of European music is to point out resemblances that are to a certain extent superficial. The phraseology of jazz is related to a wholly different functional plan, characteristic of an art that is essentially unpredictable and impulsive.

Chapter 15

JAZZ AS A FINE ART

ALREADY IN the 1930s, when Benny Goodman was beginning to reach the height of his popularity, and the large, lush type of jazz promulgated by Paul Whiteman and others was taking on a distinctly commercialized and standard tone, a change was taking place in the attitude of jazz listeners, and this change was reflected, to some extent, in the techniques of jazz. Not that the commercial jazz band disappeared; it is still with us. But people of discrimination began to recognize jazz as an art, and to demand a certain freshness of inspiration and improvisation as its *sine qua non*. Books were written about the essential—as opposed to the commercial—type of jazz, those by Wilder Hobson and the Frenchman Hugues Panassié becoming the pioneer critical works. Researches among the personalities and recordings of the so-called New Orleans, Chicago and St. Louis styles were avidly pursued. Collections of recordings were made; standards of criticism were arrived at, and the jazz connoisseur made his appearance on the scene. Since then, of course, the literature on jazz—critical, biographical and historical—has grown to enormous proportions. Magazines devoted to the subject have flourished; jazz critics have been added to the staffs of a great many highly respected publications, and the recording of the most free and imaginative jazz has become a large business—not as large, perhaps, as the commercial turnover of routine popular records, but very extensive nevertheless. What I have referred to in the preceding chapters as "hot" jazz (the term is, of course, not mine, and it is beginning to take on a slightly archaic sound) was the focus of attention for the jazz connoisseur, but it underwent a number of much less "hot" developments that took it far beyond the boundaries of what is ordinarily called "folk music." The Negro musician, who had invented the whole thing in the first place, began to assume his proper predominance in the field, and to be celebrated and paid accordingly. Jazz departed completely from its cane brake, cotton field and brothel origins, and became, more and more, a big city phenomenon. Dancing, at least for the connoisseurs, became entirely divorced from it except, here and there, as a spectator art. The music of the old-time "shoutin'" congregation (though it undoubtedly survives in some environments) passed from the picture as the connoisseurs saw it, leaving only an exaggerated remnant known as "gospel singing." Modern jazz arose to fill the requirements of a new generation of urbane auditors.

The change was by no means abrupt. Classics of primitive jazz were still revered. The astonishingly durable Duke Ellington has survived it, and so (at this writing) have Louis Armstrong, Jack Teagarden and others. It is one of the peculiarities of our time that history has become foreshortened, and eclecticism prevails. Styles change with bewildering rapidity, so fast, indeed, that one finds many a "historical figure" still at work while the most "progressive" exponents of every art are striking at new horizons. And the word "progressive" is somewhat deceptive here too, since no art really progresses, but, on the contrary, merely changes superficially to fit into successive styles. Ellington's sensitive orchestrations and compositions, and Armstrong's robust trumpet playing, do not really belong to the past; they are still around, and, in Ellington's case, as good as or better than ever. But there have been certain stylistic developments since the original heyday of these musicians that have given some types of jazz a new and different sound. The anatomical principles deduced in the preceding chapters still hold for the bulk of jazz, but, in some quarters, experiments have taken place which depart from the jazz "language" as I have described it.

In general, these new developments are the result of changed sociological conditions which have brought the educated Negro into contact with more complicated types of music. Many present-day jazz performers are graduates of established conservatories of music, where they have learned all the tricks of "classical" composition and performance. And, in a reciprocal way, it is true that today many a "classical" American concert performer can improvise jazz—something that his forebears of a generation ago were unable to do. Courses in jazz are now part of the curriculum of many music schools. Integration between Negroes and Whites—a phenomenon that showed an emotional premonition in music long before it appeared anywhere else—is now closer than ever. Jazz, as I have already pointed out, is a Negro contribution to music—if one practiced, sometimes with considerable artistry, by Whites. It has, however, always contained European ingredients, particularly in the realm of harmony. Today, the European ingredients are by no means less. They are, in fact, greater in a good deal of modern jazz, and they are so because the jazz player has become an adept in the techniques of conventional "classical" music. The other sociological changes are even more apparent. Jazz, nowadays, is performed at huge music festivals like the annual one at Newport; it is sent abroad on world tours as an exhibit of American culture; it is imitated by European and Asian ensembles, and written about by pundits in those regions. Its Americanization—if one can call its spread to all colors and types of Americans that—is being followed by internationalization. It is going great guns in Japan. It has even invaded Soviet Russia, and probably will someday be heard in Communist China. Just how far it has come from its "African" origins is indicated by Louis Armstrong's remark, after a recent tour of Africa, that, though he was greeted everywhere with enormous enthusiasm, the inhabitants didn't really "dig" his music.

It has been contended by Henry Pleasants, the author of *The Agony of Modern Music*, that the great tradition of eighteenth and nineteenth century opera and concert music is dead, and that jazz had arisen to take its place. I do not agree with Pleasants on this point, for a number of reasons, among them that the White man's music is still very much alive in certain areas like the Broadway musical show, which has little or nothing to do with jazz, and even in some pretty good contemporary operas, symphonies and concertos. There certainly has been a decline, however, in the general quality of symphonic and operatic composition in Europe, and there has been an increasing interest there in jazz. To me, one is no substitute for the other. When I go to hear Joan Sutherland sing in a Bellini opera, or Leontine Price in a Verdi or Puccini one—or when I go to hear a Barber concerto or a Shostakovich symphony—the emotional experience I undergo is quite different from what I receive in listening to a jazz ensemble; and I am not ready to concede the total defeat of an elaborate, magnificently planned art which has persisted for at least three centuries in something like its present form and is still being avidly pursued, even though, at the moment, the creative side of this art has fallen into a state of decline. There is no doubt, however, that jazz has reached a peak of popularity (with an entirely different public) at the very point where the "highbrow" composer seems to have run out of steam, and I should be the last to deny the freshness and inspiration of jazz in this crucial era of history, in comparison with the enfeeblement of the more complex art of Europe. Moreover, some highbrow composers at the moment—Lukas Foss and Gunther Schuller among others—are seeking to introduce the phenomenon of group improvisation into symphonic writing. Jazz symphonies (i.e., symphonies with jazz themes and rhythms) are now somewhat old hat. Foss and Schuller are attempting to get into symphonic music not the themes, but the very aesthetic method of jazz. An interesting experiment, but not, judging by what I have heard, a very fruitful one so far.

Starting from the other end, however, things are a great deal more absorbing. The jazz musician, now more educated than heretofore in the mysteries of the conservatoire and the concert hall, has, since the last war, again been influenced by European music, and by a more recent stream of European music than the hymn tunes and marches that inspired the Negroes of the old South. I remind you again that we are in the midst of a period of historical foreshortening. Chronology, as applied to recent jazz, is almost meaningless. There are layers of contemporary jazz that reflect all the robustness of the "Chicago" style, and do not depart from it in any important respect except perhaps a tendency toward more fragmented melody. But there are also other layers in which jazz has taken on the characteristic evolutionary development of European music, as exemplified in the whole-tone-scale impressionism of Debussy, a certain amount of chromaticism, and finally the atonality of Schönberg and Bartok. This evolution has not been so much the result of anything within jazz itself as a product of the study of European music by jazz musicians, and whether it is really an evolution or a sign of weakness in jazz can be debated. Jazz, at any rate, has been influenced by what, in highbrow circles, is called "modern music"—and why not, considering that plenty of jazz musicians go to concerts where it is performed and attended music schools where it is taught? Jazz has also been conspicuously influenced by the vogue for the modern "baroque" ensemble, from which we nowadays hear seventeenth and eighteenth-century music more clearly, gently and accurately performed than it was in the recent past. We have learned that music is not necessarily greater because it is louder, and the jazz composer and performer have, to some extent, adopted the same view. The result, in many quarters, has been a move toward refinement, a chamber-music style and a greater delicacy of musical fabric, and along with this has come a more sophisticated kind of playing. At the same time, another element, previously unknown in jazz, has entered the picture, namely "form" as it applies to more complex structures than the variation, or such variations of the variation as the chaconne and passacaglia, into which categories much earlier jazz fell. The variation form is an open-ended one: it could go on indefinitely; it has no inevitable conclusion as a symphony or a concerto has. When one got tired of making variations one simply stopped playing, as one might finish a conversation on an exhausted subject. Most early jazz had this episodic structure and hence was incapable of the architectural climaxes, intense conscious organization, and dramatic proportion of "classical" music. Nowadays, however, the jazz musician has learned all about form. He creates jazz fugues and preludes; he even manages jazz in waltz time, though these procedures inevitably lead to boundaries beyond which jazz passes over into something else.

Let us examine the results of this progress, if so it may be called. Bebop, whose development is generally credited to the late Charlie Parker and to Dizzie Gillespie—and its later variant Hard Bop—brought to jazz a new, rapid, staccato and rather fiery character which is thought be some to reflect the tensions of the second World War. Its emphasis was different from that of the jazz that had preceded it. It broke the conventions of the rigid, foursquare thirty-two bar chorus; it introduced a greater degree of chromaticism, and even flirted, on occasion, with the whole-tone scale. On the whole, however, it did not depart, in matters of harmonic and rhythmic structure, from jazz as it was known prior to the war, though, here and there, a great deal of variation from previous norms, especially in drumming, gave it a somewhat revolutionary character.

Along with Bop came "cool" jazz, as represented in the work of Miles Davis and a few others. Now, with "cool" jazz, a real revolution seems to have taken place. Tonality sometimes became ambiguous. Changes of tempo set in, allegros being interspersed with adagios. The basic beat was occasionally left out altogether, and even harmony, at times, became nonexistent. Fragmented solos were prominent. The vibraphone, or vibraharp, came into great vogue, and the general tone of small ensembles tended toward the gentle and soothing. In phase structure, there was greater variety than jazz had hitherto revealed, and, for the first time, "form," in the "classical" sense, became very evident, though "cool" jazz still retained a great deal of what—at least superficially—sounded like very free improvisation. Instrumentation became more elastic and more subtle. The robustness of earlier jazz disappeared, at least from this particular stratum of the art. Miles Davis seems to have become a sort of Claude Debussy of jazz. At any rate, in listening to such records as *Birth of the Cool* (Capitol) and *Miles Davis and the Modern Jazz Giants* (Prestige), one is often struck with the impression that what one is listening to is not jazz at all. Most of the numbers on the former disc might be the work of a "classical" impressionist composer with a great sense of aural poetry and a very fastidious feeling for tone color. The compositions have beginnings, middles and endings. The music sounds more like that of a new Maurice Ravel than it does like jazz. I, who do not listen to jazz recordings day in and day out, find this music charming and exciting. Obviously the composer and the arranger have had a large part in creating it. Effects like these do not arise from sudden impulse during performance. They have been carefully contrived, or written down, beforehand, and have all the features of "composed" music. They also introduced a "romantic" element into what had never been a particularly romantic art. I note that a number of jazz critics are finding this sort of thing a little precious. I don't want to take sides in the controversy. If Miles Davis were an established "classical" composer, his work would rank high among that of his contemporary colleagues. But it is not really jazz. It is a gesture in the direction of highbrow "classical" music, and, if it were to set a permanent trend, the boundaries between jazz and "classical" would disappear. Why shouldn't they? Maybe the boundaries *will* someday disappear, and there is certainly no reason why a gifted jazz composer, as an individual, should not turn himself into a gifted "classical" one. But if the whole art should go that way, there would be a great loss to jazz as a distinct idiom, and I doubt whether the gains in the "classical" direction would be worth it. The jazz critics undoubtedly have a point.

Then, we come to that very celebrated institution, the Modern Jazz Quartet, a remarkable, soft-spoken ensemble that can apparently sound like anything from a Couperin pavane to a symphony by Anton Bruckner, and still preserve an authentic jazz flavor. It consists, of course, of a peculiar combination of instruments—a piano, a vibraharp, a string bass and drums—which, altogether, gives out a rather ethereal sound (no brasses, no woodwinds). Its playing is extremely refined and very consciously contrived. On the other hand, what it plays is nearly always indentifiable as jazz. It sticks to the blue inflections and regular basic and superimposed rhythms far more closely than Miles Davis does. Its pianist— and I gather its leading spirit—is John Lewis, a very talented composer indeed, and one of exceedingly eclectic tastes. One finds with him, as with Davis, that one is dealing with a musician of "classical" sophistication, by which I mean that both have obviously studied and heard a great deal of "classical" music. Lewis, however, is a great ransacker of varied styles. He produces jazz fugues, jazz waltzes and little jazz concertos in a sort of jazz-baroque style. He is no folk musician. His conceptions are the outcome of influences both inside and outside jazz. He and Davis are both far more satisfying artists than ninety percent of present-day "classical" composers. They have something to say, and they say it gracefully and simply. Whether Lewis' fugues and other (I must say rather delightful) archaisms are in the main stream of jazz is for future historians to determine. There is, to my mind, something just a little too tricky about them. Also, in the compositions *Exposure* and *Sketch*, which appear on the recording entitled *Third Stream Music* —a series of works written for Lewis' group in combination with the Beaux Arts String Quartet—he can get as far away from his jazz moorings as Davis. If Bach isn't giving him ideas on one hand, Webern and Messiaen are on the other. The Modern Jazz Quartet seems capable of doing practically anything, and doing it with a satin finish. Its playing is predominantly tonal, except when it gets entangled with the highbrow atonal composer Gunther Schuller, which it does on this recording in something called *Conversation*, where it achieves a complex kind of utterance that, to me at least, lacks any spontaneity or musical meaning whatever.

Third-stream jazz, or third-stream music seems, in fact, to depend a great deal for its eloquence on which of the two old streams it branches off from. As a theory, it is Schuller's, and it is easy to see its attraction for both sides: Carnegie Hall-type prestige for the jazz artist, and a badly needed blood transfusion for the modern "classical" composer. In practice, however, it doesn't really seem to constitute a third stream. When the Modern Jazz Quartet is playing Lewis, or improvisations of a group character, it sounds like itself; in a sense, perhaps both Miles Davis and Lewis had already evolved a third stream before Schuller put a label to it. When Schuller himself is imposed on the Modern Jazz Quartet, however, I have always found the result to be so constricted, inhibited and self-conscious that spontaneity, imagination and human communication become almost impossible.

And here we come to the last development of this stratum —atonal jazz—last because one cannot go beyond it into anything else. In "classical" music, atonality has stood in a state of more or less rigid paralysis for half a century. It may have its amusing features as an arcane game played among musicians. But it has never, since Arnold Schönberg evolved it, added anything to music as a living expression. And the worst feature of it is its blind-alley character. It leads nowhere except to more atonality. It is the end of progress. It is the sinking ship from which Mr. Pleasants hoped that jazz would rescue music, and Ornette Coleman and the pianist Cecil Taylor seem, at times, to be lashing themselves to its deck. Taylor, a graduate of a couple of "classical" conservatories, is obviously a musician of technical accomplishment who has studied all the methods of highbrow modern music. The prevalence of jazz rhythm in his work gives it a vestige of vitality. But his playing contains the germs that could, one day, spell the death of jazz, just as Schönberg's atonality pretty much spelled the death of "classical" music, viewed as an evolving art. Coleman, an alto saxophonist and disciple of Charlie Parker, has a more intuitive and uncalculated approach, but his results do not seem to me very different, except where orchestration is concerned.

Fortunately, I think, the main stream of jazz continues to spring from its original sources in the work of many artists still before the public, and also continues, with all its intensity and verve, in the playing of such more recent figures as Sonny Rollins and Bill Evans. Fads continue to come and go. It would be too much to expect that the modern, highly educated jazz musician would not, at one time or another, latch onto some technical feature of the "classical" decadence. But jazz is, in some ways, fortunate to be bound to its folk music origins, and to a robust form of popular band music, which, though often routine and uninteresting in itself, nevertheless serves as an anchor of tradition from which individual artists may stray, but to which they are always entitled to return.

Meanwhile, let me make a few points about modern jazz in general. Inevitably it is becoming a literate art as opposed to the folk music that jazz once was. I suspect that its ventures into atonality are a fad of the moment. But the polished character of nearly all of today's small band music has brought deliberate composition and rehearsal into a much more prominent position than they occupied in the more or less purely improvised music of the pre-war period. Its present-day composers and arrangers are nearly all Negroes, and what they compose and arrange has a spontaneity that was lacking in the routine, big-band arrangements of the Fletcher Henderson and Benny Goodman dance-band era. What the future holds is difficult to foresee and idle to prophesy. Education in "classical" musical technique is both a source of intellectual interest and a threat to jazz as a distinct type of music. Maybe the third stream is the stream of the future, but if jazz is to remain a vital art, its vitality will depend mainly on Negro composers, arrangers and performers. After all, as I have said before, it is *their* music.

Just how indisputably this is the case has very recently been demonstrated by A. M. Jones in his monumental work "Studies in African Music" (Oxford University Press, London, 1959). In this painstaking and scholarly work, we now have that comprehensive survey of musical Africa the absence of which I lamented in Chapter 12. Jones' studies rest mainly on material he has collected in Northern Rhodesia and Ghana, but he has been in most parts of Africa, and he offers pretty convincing proof that the African musical language is more or less the same everywhere south of the Sahara, regardless of linguistic differences. The exceptions to this rule seem to occur only where Moslem influence is prominent, and where contact with Western music, in large cities, has produced a "neo-folk music" which is a little like jazz, but evidently far less interesting. Jones' two volumes are fairly exhaustive, and the amount of transcription of native material into Western notation verges on the heroic. The music he has transcribed in isolated villages is a great deal freer in rhythm than jazz, and, indeed, shows a native rhythmic instinct far surpassing that of any Western musician, jazz or highbrow. But it is interesting to note, in connection with this music, that the three over four superimposition characteristic of jazz is to be found luxuriating all over the place, though Jones' habit of scoring the contrapuntal rhythms of African music on separate staves with non-coincident bar lines and different time signatures makes this point difficult to detect except by the trained musician. African music, judging from Jones' examples, also contains a rich store of other types of syncopation, if one means by that term the displacement of a basic rhythm. His method of notating African music on different staves with different time signatures is obviously the only one practicable for music of such freely polyrhythmic character, and after studying his extended examples, one is overcome by the rhythmic elasticity, subtlety, inventiveness and logic of the African musical mind. Regularity of rhythm in the Western sense is apparently regarded by the African as unimaginative, if not downright bad taste. His musical instinct is to displace the basic beat—and for two African musicians to pound, sing or dance in rhythmic consonance with one another is at least highly exceptional. His music shows a continuous variety of rhythmic pattern, piled up in as many as five or six distinct contrapuntal voices, and he seems to evolve his skill in doing this sort of thing at an early age. Here, we are undoubtedly face to face with one of the two musical languages out of which jazz has grown, and the African musical language is far more complex, rhythmically, than jazz is. Unfortunately, as Jones points out, the authentic African musical language is already dying out (the universal fate of non-European folk music in the era of phonographs and radios), and is to be found, today, only in the more primitive areas of the continent.

Harmonically, this music bears some relation to jazz. Blue notes are a feature of it, but Jones has found that, where harmonic feeling in our sense can be discerned in it at all, the only striking feature is a dominant-sharped subdominant-dominant sequence which is not characteristic of jazz. There are several features of African music, however, that are, on the abstract plane, similar to features of jazz. Jones enumerates them on page 49 of Volume 1 (quite properly without any reference to jazz) as follows: "1) The songs [of Africa] appear to be in free rhythm, but most of them have a fixed time background. 2) The rule of 2 and 3 in the metrical build of a song. 3) Nearly all rhythms which are used in combination are made from simple aggregations of a basic time unit. 4) The claps, or other time-background, impart no accent whatever to the song. 5) African melodies are additive—their time background is divisive. 6) The principle of cross rhythms. 7) The rests within and at the end of a song before repeats are an integral part of it. 8) Repeats are an integral part of the song; they result in many variations of the call and response form. 9) The call and response type of song is usual in Africa. 10) African melodies are diatonic—the major exception being the sequence dominant-sharped subdominant-dominant. 11) Short triplets are occasionally used. 12) The teleological trend: many African songs lean towards the *ends* of the lines, where they are likely to coincide with their time background. 13) Absence of the *fermata*." Elsewhere he remarks that "changes of speed are not usual in African music."

Now, bearing in mind that the music he is writing about is quite different from jazz, still, in looking over this list of characteristics, it is quite obvious that, in the abstract (i.e., as general principles of structure), all of them, except possibly No. 2, are characteristic of jazz as well as African music—far apart though the two may be in many respects. From Jones' admirable study, we can now at least guess at the process by which the Negro, faced with, and incorporating, various features of the popular and religious music of the American Whites, formed his distinct American musical dialect. The foursquare Western phraseology, the regularity of Western rhythm and the possibilities of Western harmony may have seemed either limiting or stimulating, as the case may be. But the American Negro, in grafting his African musical language onto that of the Whites, still managed to preserve some features of his original aesthetic scheme, and the result was jazz —an entirely new contribution to the art of music.

Chapter 16

CONCLUSIONS

SOMETIME AGO in a speech the late James Weldon Johnson remarked sardonically that where music and dancing are concerned, Americans are always "doing their best to pass for colored." The presence of African idioms in the bulk of our popular music, the instinctive manner in which even the White American musician turns to jazz improvisation, the spontaneous response of the average American to jazz as something that "speaks his own language," something that "feels" even more akin to him than the prim songs of his European forbears—these things all hint at profound ethnological questions that the present writer is scarcely qualified to tackle.

It is obvious, nevertheless, that jazz does respond in several ways to what is loosely spoken of as the "American psychology"; that while its ancestry may be African and European, it is none the less a peculiarly American form of musical expression. The spontaneous, improvisatory aspect of jazz is remarkably adapted to the musical needs of a pragmatic, pioneering people. Like the typical American, the jazz musician goes his own syncopated way, making instantaneous and novel adjustments to problems as they present themselves. He is an individualist. He prefers making his own kind of music to interpreting the compositions of sanctified masters. He is little concerned with precedent and is inclined to respect what "works" rather than what is laid down in theory books. The discipline of tradition "cramps his style." He cannot abide the idea of foregone conclusions: an art form that demands a beginning, a middle and an inevitable end is alien to his psychology. His greatest "kick" is gotten out of feverish activity; his goal is usually somewhat indefinite.

It is not surprising that a society that has evolved the skyscraper, the baseball game, and the "happy ending" movie, should find its most characteristic musical expression in an art like jazz. Contrast a skyscraper with a Greek temple or a mediaeval cathedral. Where each of the latter gives forth a sense of repose, of acceptance, of catharsis, the skyscraper thrusts unrestrainedly upward. Its height is not limited by considerations of form—but by the momentary limits of practical engineering. Where the Greek temple and the cathedral are built for permanence, the skyscraper is soon torn down and replaced by taller and better skyscrapers. The individual skyscraper is merely a tentative makeshift. Another generation will probably relegate it to the junk heap, a fact of which its designers and builders are fully aware. Like the jazz "composition" it is an impermanent link in a continuous process. And, like jazz, the skyscraper lacks the restraint and poise of the classical tradition. The skyscraper has a beginning (*i.e.*, a foundation) and perhaps a middle, but its end is an indefinite upward thrust. A jazz performance ends, not because of the demands of musical logic, but because the performers or listeners are tired, or wish to turn to something else for a change. It lacks entirely the element of dramatic climax. As far as form is concerned it might end equally well at the finish of almost any of its eight-bar phrases. A skyscraper ends its upward thrust in a somewhat analogous way. It might be stopped at almost any point in its towering series of floors. It must, of course, stop somewhere. But the stop is not made primarily for reasons of proportion. Nor does it carry that sense of inevitableness that attaches to the height of the Greek temple. It stops simply because its builders didn't have money enough, or energy enough to make it still higher, or because the practicalities of big city life made greater height inadvisable.

The same analogy can be carried over into the field of popular drama where the American preference for "happy endings" is found in more than nine out of ten movies and radio scripts. What is the "happy ending"? A kiss, a vague promise of future joy—in other words, no ending at all. The typical American does not like endings. He is an incurable progressive. He does not like to bother his head thinking about doom and destiny. There is something about inevitability that runs contrary to his conception of life. And because of this his most characteristic arts—the comic strip, the skyscraper, journalism, jazz, the tap dance, the "happy ending" movie—all lack the element of "form" that is so essential to tragedy, to the symphony, to the novel, to the opera, to monumental architecture and even to some of the less pretentious arts of other nations. These remarks are not made in any spirit of belittlement toward what are, after all, America's popular "lowbrow" arts. The lowbrow arts of other lands are often less interesting and less vital than America's. The point is that America's lowbrow arts seem to be her most characteristic ones. Her novels, symphonies, plays and churches are all more or less closely related to European prototypes. Her popular art is not.

The difference between a jazz performance and a classical "composition" is not only a difference in musical substance. It reflects a difference in national psychology. The European "composition" is a complex structure of organized sound, fixed more or less immutably as to form. It perpetuates the message of a creative mind through generations, even centuries. The understanding of this message presupposes a tradition—a guarantee that men will, to some extent, think and feel alike from generation to generation. The form in which this message is cast is subject to a process of intellectual development. Its composers themselves are highly trained professionals, the greatest of them capable of extraordinary feats of technique which average people marvel at but can scarcely hope to duplicate.

Jazz lacks these conditions and attributes. It relies on suspense, on sudden adjustments to the unexpected, for its essential vitality. The best of it is created impulsively, and is forgotten almost instantly afterward. Its tradition is not a carefully guarded intellectual heritage, but a simple matter of musical instinct. From its listeners, jazz invites not contemplation or applause, but participation. It is a "get together" art for "regular fellows," a breaker down of social and psychological barriers, an expression not of aristocratic craftsmanship but of mass good fellowship.

A great deal of recent writing about jazz has assumed for it the status of a fine art. The eloquent defenders of *"le jazz hot"* have held jazz concerts in the most impressively conservative American concert halls, and have discussed these concerts in lofty critical language. They have written books and published magazines dealing solemnly with the aesthetics of jazz and the artistry of the popular virtuosos who play it. They have even argued that the great musical issue of the day is that of jazzism vs. "classicism," that jazz is in some way the American successor to the venerable art of concert music, its tunesmiths and improvising virtuosos the latter-day equivalents of so many

JAZZ: HOT AND HYBRID

Beethovens and Wagners. Bach, after all, used to improvise too.

The enormous popularity of jazz, coupled with the prevailing decadence of concert and operatic music, has given this view a superficial appearance of weight. Considered merely as a social phenomenon jazz leaves its unfriendly critics in the position of King Canute. You can't ignore an art that makes up seventy per cent of the musical diet of a whole nation, even if its primitive thumps and wails fail to fit the aesthetic categories of refined music criticism. Jazz has often been innocently described as a "folk music." And, considered purely as music, it is one. But its powers over the common man's psyche are not even vaguely suggested by that term. No other folk music in the world's history has ever induced among normal people such curious psychopathic aberrations as the desire to wear a zoot suit, smoke hashish or jabber cryptic phrases of "jive" language. None, probably, has ever produced waves of mass hysteria among adolescents like those recently associated with the swing craze. Nor has any folk music ever before constituted the mainstay of half a dozen nation-wide publishing, recording, broadcasting and distributing industries.

Yet when you try to approach jazz from a critical point of view, you are immediately struck by a curious split which divides almost every aspect of jazz from any real correspondence with so-called "classical" music. For all the attempts of Paul Whiteman, Benny Goodman and others to bridge the gap, it still remains generally true that jazz players can't play "classical," and that "classical" players can't play jazz. Not one jazz *aficionado* in a thousand has any interest in "classical" music, and very few serious concertgoers feel anything more cordial than mild irritation when they listen to jazz. Attempted mixtures of the two idioms invariably act like oil and water. Jazzed classics and symphonies with jazz themes have a tendency to ruffle tempers in both camps. Even the impartial critic is at a loss for any similar scale of standards in the two arts. Though many a jazz aesthete has tried to, you can't compare a Louis Armstrong solo to a Josef Szigeti sonata performance, or a Bessie Smith blues to an aria from *Rigoletto*. There isn't any common ground.

The disregard of this distinction among jazz critics has led to some curious concert ventures and to a vast amount of amazing aesthetic double-talk. Jazz concerts in Carnegie Hall and the Metropolitan Opera House have been hailed as cultural milestones when, in fact, they only proved that jazz can be played in uncongenial surroundings especially designed for the wholly different requirements of *Traviata* or the New York Philharmonic—if that needed proving. Ever since the pundit Hugues Panassie discovered *le jazz hot* in a French chateau full of phonograph records, the world of intellectual jazz addicts has been calling a spade a *cuiller à caviar*. The ebullient, hit-or-miss ensemble of a New Orleans stomp is reverently described as "counterpoint"; the jazz trumpeter's exuberant and raucous lapses from true pitch are mysteriously referred to as "quarter tones" or "atonality." Jazz, as an art with a capital A, has become something to be listened to with a rapt air that would shame the audiences of the Budapest Quartet. To dance to it (which is just what its primitive Negro originators would do) becomes a profanation.

Highbrow composers have also tried bridging the gap. The idea that an amalgamation of jazz with such traditional forms as the sonata or the symphony might result in an American style of concert music is too attractive to be ignored. American composers have repeatedly written jazz symphonies, jazz concertos and jazz fugues. But they usually discard the idea after a few experiments, and they never succeed in using jazz as anything but a superficial ornamental embellishment, as they might, say, use a Balinese or Algerian tune for local color. Their so-called jazz composition is not jazz at all—as any jitterbug can tell from the first note. Its rigid highbrow musical structure prohibits the very type of improvisation that makes jazz fun to listen to. It remains a "classical" composition with jazz-style trimmings, something about as American and about as homogeneous as a Greek temple with a shingle roof. The outstanding exception to this rule is probably Gershwin's mildly jazzy opera *Porgy and Bess*, which came close to artistic success. But Gershwin's opera is saved, as far as the appropriateness of its music is concerned, mainly because it is a folk opera with a Negro setting. It is, in other words, a highly specialized type of opera, if, indeed, it can properly be considered an opera at all. The use of the same idiom in connection with the generality of operatic drama would be unthinkable.

Why does this peculiar split exist? The answer, I think, will be found by clearing away the pseudo-classical verbiage of the jazz critic and looking at the aesthetic nature of jazz itself. Jazz, for all the enthusiasms of its intellectual *aficionados,* is not music in the sense that an opera or a symphony is music. It is a variety of folk music. And the distinction between folk music and art music is profound and nearly absolute. The former grows like a weed or a wildflower, exhibits no intellectual complexities, makes a simple, direct emotional appeal that may be felt by people who are not even remotely interested in music as an art. It is often beautiful to listen to, whether it is jazz, or Irish or Welsh ballad singing, or Spanish *flamenco* guitar playing, or New England sea chanties, or Venetian gondolier songs. But it is not subject to intellectual criticism, for it lacks the main element toward which such criticism would be directed: the creative ingenuity and technique of an unusual, trained musical mind.

Art music, on the other hand, is an art as complicated as architecture. It begins where folk music leaves off, in the conscious creation of musical edifices that bear the stamp, in style and technique, of an individual artist. Its traditions—the rules of its game—are complicated and ingenious. They are the result of centuries of civilized musical thinking by highly trained musicians for audiences that are capable of judging the finer points of such thought. Art music is no field of wildflowers. It is a hothouse of carefully bred and cultivated masterpieces, each one the fruit of unusual talent and great technical resourcefulness. You may prefer the open fields of folk music to the classical hothouse. That is your privilege. But if so, you are simply not interested in music as a fine art. And it is no use getting snobbish about your preference and pretending that your favorite musical wildflower is a masterpiece of gardening skill. It isn't.

Thus, the remarks "I prefer early Chicago-style jive to *Tristan and Isolde*," or "I prefer Kirsten Flagstad to Ethel Waters" are not really critical or evaluative statements. They are like saying "I prefer percherons to race horses"—an understandable preference, but one that would be meaningless to a racing enthusiast. "But after all, hasn't jazz got melody, rhythm and harmony, and aren't these attributes of concert music?" Of course. But the uses to which these materials are put differ greatly in the two arts. Jazz harmony, as we have seen, is restricted to four or five monotonous patterns which support the florid improvisations of the soloist like a standardized scaffolding. These patterns never differ, never make any demands on creative ingenuity. Virtually every blues, and every piece of boogie woogie pianism, uses precisely the same harmony as every other blues or boogie woogie piece. Rhythmically, jazz is somewhat more ingenious, but not much more varied. It is limited to four-four or two-four time, and its most interesting effects are the result of blind instinct rather than thought.

Melodically, jazz is often strikingly beautiful and original. But jazz melody, like all folk melody, is of the amoebic rather than the highly organized type. Jazz melody, unlike most highbrow melody, consist of tunes rather than themes. These tunes are as simple and self-contained as one-cell animals. They can be repeated, sometimes with embellishments and variations, but they are incapable of being formed into higher musical organisms. Cell for cell, or melody for melody, they often compare favorably with the themes of highbrow music. The melody of Bessie Smith's *Cold in Hand Blues,* for example, is a much more beautiful tune than the "V for Victory" theme of Beethoven's *Fifth Symphony.* But when you have played it, that is all there is—a beautiful, self-sufficient amoeba. Beethoven's crusty little motif is a cell of a different sort, almost without significance by itself, but capable of being reproduced into a vast symphonic organism with dramatic climaxes and long range emotional tensions.

The jazz artist, like all folk musicians, creates his one-cell melodies by instinct and repeats them over and over again, perhaps with simple variations. The composer of art music, on the other hand, is interested in one-cell melodies only as raw material. His creative mind begins where the instinct of the folk musician leaves off, in building such material into highly organized forms like symphonies and fugues. It is the technique and ingenuity with which he accomplishes this job that is the main subject of music criticism, as it applies to composition. And this is why music criticism is apt to sound pompous and miss its mark when it is applied to the creative side of a folk art like jazz. There is, to be sure, a large amount of concert music and of opera that is related to folk-music sources, and that sometimes scarcely rises above the folk-music level. Chopin waltzes, Brahms Hungarian dances, Tchaikovsky ballet tunes, Grieg songs, old-fashioned Italian operatic arias, and so on, sometimes fall under this heading. But the sophisticated music world has long thought of these items as belonging to a special, "semi-popular" category. They are not the backbone of symphonic or operatic art. And they are seldom the subject of serious music criticism.

One of the most striking features of jazz as compared with art music is its lack of evolutionary development. Aside from a few minor changes of fashion, its history shows no technical evolution whatever. The formulas of the jazz musical language that we have analyzed were nearly all used in the earliest of jazz and still constitute, with minor modifications, the basis of jazz technique. Occasionally, as in the piano rag, these formulas have taken on a special character due to the popularity of certain instruments or combinations of instruments. But the formulas themselves have remained constant. Jazz today remains essentially the same kind of music it was in 1900. Its simple forms—the blues, the eight-bar barbershop phrases—have been characteristic of it from the very beginning. This lack of evolution, which is an attribute of all folk music, is another of the main differences between jazz and concert music. The history of the latter shows a continuous development of structural methods. Few important highbrow composers have left the technique of music where they found it.

Considered as performance, jazz has more impressive claims to critical attention. Its virtuoso performers are often gifted with extraordinary technique of a sort, and are nearly always differentiated by interesting individualities of style. Jazz performance has its own type of excitement. But it is a totally different type of excitement from what one feels when listening to a performance of concert music. In the concert hall or opera house, music is not only an art but a kind of game. The soprano singing the most hackneyed coloratura aria (or the conductor leading the profoundest symphony) sets about overcoming certain pre-arranged obstacles of which the audience is aware. There is a special exhilaration (more or less independent of purely musical pleasure) in noting the ease with which the soprano hits her high notes, or the suavity and polish with which she turns her melodic phrases. It is like watching a crack shot on a complicated target range, making an extraordinary number of bullseyes. This particular exhilaration is completely lacking in jazz. There are no obstacles, no precise tests of technical mastery. Inspired by his mood, the improvising jazz player may launch into quite remarkable feats of virtuosity. But the virtuosity all appears on the spur of the moment, some of it the result of sudden emotion, some even the result of accident. Since he is improvising, one is never quite sure what the player set out to do in the first place. One doesn't know which target he is shooting at.

The much-discussed element of improvisation, too, has been greatly overrated in recent writing about jazz. A false impression has been given that the jazz artist, when he is "in the groove," creates an entirely new musical composition extemporaneously. Actually this is never the case. Only a small portion of the jazz heard today is improvised. And even in that small portion improvisation affects only a few elements of rhythm and melody. The two most intellectually complex features of music—harmony and form—are never improvised even in so-called improvised jazz. They conform in every case to well-worn standard patterns.

Perhaps the most artistically significant peculiarity of jazz as opposed to "classical" music, however, is the extremely limited nature of its emotional vocabulary. As a musical language, jazz is graphic and colorful, but in poetic resources it is about as rich as pidgin English. A great deal of it appeals exclusively to the motor impulses without affecting the emotions at all. When it does affect the emotions, it is limited to the expression of a few elementary moods—sexual excitement, exhilaration, sorrow (in the blues), and a sort of hypnotic intoxication. Its vocabulary does not encompass religious awe, tragedy, romantic nostalgia, metaphysical contemplation, grandeur, wonder, patriotic or humanitarian fervor—all of them more or less stock-in-trade emotions conveyed or embellished by highbrow symphonic or operatic music. A jazz finale to Beethoven's *Ninth Symphony,* a jazz *Funeral March* in *Götterdämmerung* or a jazz *Pelleas et Melisande* would impose considerable strain on the expressive powers of jazz, not to speak of the artistic sensibilities of the listener.

These comparisons between jazz and the traditional art of the concert hall and opera house may strike the musically sophisticated reader as being somewhat obvious. But the confusion they attempt to clarify has befogged a tremendous amount of contemporary journalism. The more you analyze the aesthetic

peculiarities of jazz the more you realize that it is completely
unlike any other type of music that has ever existed. Musically,
it is really something new under the sun. Its perennial growth
from shantytown and the canebrakes to Hollywood and the
music factories of the industrial era is something peculiar, apparently, to the kind of civilization we live in. It seems to
sprout in cycles. Every twenty years or so the American intelligentsia discovers the primitive music of the American Negro,
gives some manifestation of it a new name (ragtime, jazz, hot
jazz, swing) and begins hurling gauntlets and breaking lances
in its defense. As a rule, the type or facet of jazz that causes
this flurry is soon absorbed into the main body of commonplace,
commercial popular music and is imitated and repeated until
the intelligentsia itself gets tired of it. Then, a few years later,
some aesthete comes across the obscure wellspring of jazz again,
calls attention to it, and the process is repeated. The cycle is
usually the same. It begins with the discovery that the obscure,
uneducated Negro is playing a wonderfully engaging type of
music. It passes from discovery to exploitation. The musical
Negro is written about, moved from his humble surroundings
into the limelight, made into a self-conscious artist, paid
homage and given, if he is lucky, something in the way of
commercial success. With success comes wholesale imitation by
the popular music business, which always knows a good thing
when it sees it. The Negro's music becomes a national fad.
But this commercialization always seems to end by cheapening
and standardizing the product, and by killing the fresh, exuberant quality that the Negro originally gave it. The cycle closes
in decadence and atrophy. The Negro, like as not, goes back
to working in a garage or a cotton field, and the commercial
music business goes on manufacturing the sort of pseudo-

Negroid music that "sells" to the uncritical mass of American listeners.

If this cycle proves anything, it is that folk music is still created by a "folk"—that is, by a humble, uneducated group of peasant-like people who have been denied access to the benefits of modern civilization. It can be lifted out of its folk *melieu* and exploited commercially. But in the process it takes on a mass-production finish and loses the hand-hewn quality that gave it its original charm. It ceases to be a folk music, properly speaking, and becomes a "popular" music instead. This distinction between folk and "popular" music would have been incomprehensible to the peoples of Europe a century ago. "Popular" music is a distinctly democratic, and pretty distinctly an American, phenomenon. The age-old European class distinctions entailed a more or less permanent proletariat, or peasant class. Folk music was the music of the peasants. Art music was for the upper classes. Democracy has somehow changed this picture. It has brought about the new category of "popular" music. Popular music is mass-produced music, created, like bathtubs, automobiles or Grand Rapids furniture, to fill the needs of the average bourgeois American. Like most of the things created to fill this need, it is efficient, standardized, sometimes inspired, but usually lacking in individuality and artistic distinction. It usually gets its artistic coloring, as does most Grand Rapids furniture, by nostalgically imitating various established styles. This imitation often takes a nationalistic turn. Popular music imitates primitive Negro jazz, for example, very much as popular furniture imitates American "antiques," and with much the same result. The original primitive music of the American Negro, however, is not an antiquarian style. It is still with us. And it is so largely because the Negro, in America, still occupies the position of a small, peasant proletariat, in the old European sense. This peasant proletariat happens to have astonishing musical gifts, and, being a peasant proletariat, it is incessantly creating a true, modern folk music. We have other small regional proletariats— Tennessee hillbillies and Southwestern cowhands, for example. All of them create folk music. But it happens that the Negro is the largest and most sharply defined of all these groups. The type of music he creates is directly related to his position in American society.

The folk dialect of jazz, like any verbal dialect, was developed originally by people who were isolated from standardized education. One of its most important ingredients has been the rather colorful awkwardness—the lack of technical polish—with which it has been played. What the jazz aesthete admires in early Chicago jazz is something analogous to the naïveté of primitive painting. And this naïveté, when genuine, is the fruit of ignorance. No amount of "blackface" imitation by sophisticated musicians can really reproduce it. Jazz appeared in the first place because the poor Southern Negro couldn't get a regular musical education, and decided to make his own home-made kind of music without it. As his lot improves, and with it his facilities for musical education, he may well be attracted by both the greater slickness of American "popular" music, and the greater technical and emotional scope of "classical" music. The Negro, after all, has already proved that he can sing opera as well as blues, and compose symphonies as well as boogie woogie. It is not at all unlikely that the education of the mass of American Negroes will sound the death knell of the type of primitive jazz that the aesthetes most admire.

In spite of pure aesthetic thinking, art has a way of fitting itself to the needs of society, and society is changing pretty rapidly. Three hundred years ago, most important highbrow music (aside from the opera) was performed in churches, and the dominant forms of highbrow music were the mass and the sacred oratorio. When the concert hall supplanted the church as a place to listen to music, new forms—the symphony, the sonata and the concerto—were evolved to fill the new need. Today the future of the concert hall is in doubt. The radio and the phonograph have enormously changed the way in which the majority of people listen to music. The day of the symphony may possibly be drawing to a close, and new forms better suited to broadcasting and recording may now be in process of evolution. Already the flexible idiom of jazz has found a strong foothold in the technologically changed situation. The phonograph has made possible for the first time the preservation of composerless music. Improvisation may now be recorded in wax just as permanently as deliberately composed music was ever recorded in printed notes. Hot jazz, the composerless art, has flourished under the new dispensation.

Jazz, as I have tried to point out earlier in this chapter, has not proved itself an art of sufficient poetic or intellectual scope to take the place in civilized society occupied by the great art of concert and operatic music. But in both its "folk" and its "popular" forms, it is an art to be reckoned with. It has the quality of vitality that characterizes music designed to fill a real and thirsty demand. It has more of this vitality than a great deal of contemporary highbrow music has. Even the popular tunes of such commercial tunesmiths as Irving Berlin and Vincent Youmans convey human emotion; not as profoundly, perhaps, as Beethoven did, but clearly and understandably nevertheless. At a time when most highbrow symphonists seem conspicuously unable to convey this sort of emotion with any freshness or originality, jazz has shown a remarkable capacity for ingratiating itself with a widening musical public. Humanity will no more do without music than it will do without speech. The musical talent that produced jazz is not likely to die out. Perhaps it will someday express itself in a great art of American music. Meanwhile jazz, as a rip-snorting stimulant to the social life of a restless, energetic people, need offer no apologies. It is rapidly becoming the world's most universally welcomed popular art form. And there can be no doubt that the world is the richer for it.

BIBLIOGRAPHY

Adorno, T. W., *On Popular Music* in *Studies in Philosophy and Social Sciences*, New York, 1941, v. 9, p. 17.

Armstrong, Louis, *Swing That Music*, Longmans, Green & Co., New York, 1936.

Ballanta-Taylor, Nicholas J. G., *Jazz Music and Its Relation to African Music*, in *Musical Courier*, June 1922, New York, v. 84, No. 22, p. 7.

Ballanta-Taylor, Nicholas, J. G., *St. Helena Island Spirituals*, G. Schirmer, Inc., New York, 1925.

Baresel, Alfred, *Das Jazz-Buch*, Jul Heins. Zimmermann, Leipzig, 1926.

Baresel, Alfred, *Das Neue Jazz-Buch*. Wilhelm Zimmerman, Leipzig, 1929.

Bernhard, Paul, *Jazz, eine Musikalische Zeitfrage*, München, 1927.

Biddle, Mark, *Jazz in the School Music Program* in *School Musician*, April, 1942, New York.

Blesh, Rudi, *This is Jazz* in *Arts & Architecture*, March, April, May, June, 1944, Los Angeles.

Bolgen, Kaare A., *An Analysis of the Jazz Idiom* in *Music Teachers Review*, 1941, New York, v. 11, p. 3.

Bowman, Laura, and Antoine, Le Roy, *The Voice of Haiti*, Clarence Williams Music Publishing Co., New York.

Bragaglia, Anton Giulio, *Jazz Band*, Milano: Edizioni "Corbaccio," 1929.

Butler, Frank S., *The Master School of Professional Piano Playing*, Butler Music Co., New York, 1925.

Campos, Ruben M., *El Folklore y la Musica Mexicana*. Publicaciones de la Secretaria de Educacion Publica, Mexico City.

Chauvet, Stephen, *Musique Negre*, Paris, 1929.

JAZZ: HOT AND HYBRID

Christensen, Axel, *Axel Christensen's Instruction Book for Jazz and Novelty Piano Playing*, A. M. Christensen, Chicago, 1927.

Coeuroy, Andre, et Schaeffner, Andre, *Le Jazz*, C. Aveline, Paris, 1926.

Coeuroy, Andre, *Panorama de la Musique Contemporaine*, Kra, Paris, 1928, p. 59.

Confrey, Zez, *Modern Course in Novelty Piano Playing*, Mills Music Co., Inc., New York, 1923.

Confrey, Zez, *Ten Lessons for the Piano*, Jack Mills, Inc., New York, 1926.

Copland, Aaron, *Jazz Structure and Influence in Modern Music*, New York, January–February, 1927, p. 9.

Courlander, Harold, *Haiti Singing*, The University of North Carolina Press, Chapel Hill, N. C., 1939.

Cuney-Hare, Maud, *Negro Musicians and Their Music*, The Associated Publishers, Inc., Washington, D. C., 1936.

Curtis-Burlin, Natalie, *Songs and Tales from the Dark Continent*, New York, 1908.

Curtis-Burlin, Natalie, *Hampton Series of Negro Folk Songs*, G. Schirmer, 1918.

Daniel, Gaston, *La Musique au Congo*, in *Revue Musicale Mensuelle*, 1911, v. 7, nos. 8–9, p. 56.

Dawson, Warrington, *Le Caractere Special de la Musique Negre en Amerique* in *Societe des Americanistes*, Jour, Paris, 1932, N. S. Tome 24, p. 273.

Delaunay, Charles, *Hot Discography*, Paris, 1936. (Second edition Commodore Music Shop, New York, 1940.)

Dett, R. Nathaniel, *Religious Folk Songs of the Negro as Sung at Hampton Institute*, Hampton Institute Press, Hampton, Virginia, 1927.

Dett, R. Nathaniel, *The Emancipation of Negro Music*, in *The Southern Workman*, Hampton, Virginia, 1918, v. 47, p. 172.

Dett, R. Nathaniel, *Negro Music of the Present*, in *The Southern Workman*, Hampton, Virginia, 1918, v. 47, p. 243.

Egg, Bernhard, *Jazz Fremdwörterbuch*, Leipzig, W. Ehrler & Co., 1927.

BIBLIOGRAPHY

Eigenschenk, Edward, *Organ Jazz*, Forster Music Publishers, Inc., Chicago, 1927.

Ellis, Norman, *Instrumentation and Arranging for the Radio & Dance Orchestra*, Roell Publications, Inc., New York, 1936.

Engel, Carl, *Jazz: A Musical Discussion*, in *Atlantic Monthly*, August, 1922.

Fillmore, Henry, *Jazz Trombonist for Slide Trombone, Bass Clef*, Fillmore Music House, Cincinnati, 1919.

Fischer, Hans, *Musik und Tanz bei den Eingeboren*, in *Allegemeine Musik-Zeitung*, 1910, v. 37, no. 8, p. 418.

Fox-Strangways, A. H., *The Music of Hindostan*, Oxford University Press, 1914.

Frankenstein, Alfred V., *Syncopating Saxophones*, R. O. Ballou, Chicago, 1925.

Ganfield, Jane, *Books and Periodicals on Jazz from 1926 to 1932*, School of Library Service, Columbia University, June 6, 1933.

Gardner, Carl E., *Ragging and Jazzing, Metronome*, New York, 1919, v. 35, no. 10, p. 35.

Gilbert, Will, *Jazzmuziek: inleiding tot de Volksmuziek der Noord-Amerikaansche Negers*. 's Gravenhage: J. P. Kruseman, 1939.

Goffin, Robert, *Aux Frontieres du Jazz*, Paris: Editions du Sagittaire, 1932.

Goffin, Robert, *Jazz, from the Congo to the Metropolitan*, Doubleday Doran & Co., Garden City, New York, 1944.

Goffin, Robert, *Where Jazz Was Born*, in *Pageant*, February, 1945, New York, p. 93.

Goldberg, Isaac, *George Gershwin*, Simon & Schuster, New York, 1931.

Goldberg, Isaac, *Tin Pan Alley*, The John Day Co., New York, 1930.

Goodman, Benny, and Kolodin, Irving, *The Kingdom of Swing*, Stackpole & Sons, New York, 1939.

Gorer, Geoffrey, *Africa Dances*, Knopf, New York, 1935.

Greene, Maude, *The Background of the Beale Street Blues*, Tennessee Folklore Society, Memphis, 1941, v. 7, p. 1.

JAZZ: HOT AND HYBRID

Handy, W. C., *Blues, An Anthology,* Albert & Charles Boni, New York, 1926.

Handy, W. C., *The Birth of the Blues,* Victor Record Review, Camden, September, 1941, p. 12.

Harap, Louis, *The Case for Hot Jazz,* in *Musical Quarterly,* New York, 1941, v. 27, p. 47.

d'Harcourt, Raoul and Marguerite, *Les Musique des Incas,* Edition Geuthner, Paris, 1925.

Heinitz, Wilh., *Ueber die Musik der Somali,* in *Zeitschrift für Musikwissenschaft,* 1920, Jahrg., 2, p. 257.

Hill, Edward Burlingame, *Jazz,* in *Harvard Graduates Magazine,* Boston, 1926, v. 34, p. 362.

Hobson, Wilder, *American Jazz Music,* W. W. Norton, New York, 1939.

Hobson, Wilder, Article *Jazz* in *Encyclopedia Britannica.*

Hoeree, Arthur, *Le Jazz,* in *Revue Musicale,* Paris, 1928, Annee 8, p. 213.

Hoeree, Arthur, *Le Jazz et la Musique d'Aujourd'hui,* in *Cahiers de Belgique,* Bruxelles, 1929, Annee 2, p. 108.

Hoeree, Arthur, *Le Jazz et son Influence sur la Musique d'Aujourd'hui,* in *Menestrel,* Paris, 1929, Annee 91, p. 361.

Hornböstel, Erich M. von, *Gesänge aus Ruanda,* in *Deutsche Zentral Africa Expedition, Wissenschaftliche Ergebnisse,* Bd. 6, Teil 1, p. 379.

Hornböstel, Erich M. von, *African Negro Music,* in *International Institute of African Languages and Cultures,* Memo. 4.

Howe, Martin, *Blue Jazz,* Bristol: The Perpetua Press, 1934.

Idelsohn, A. Z., *Gesänge der Jemenischen Juden,* Benjamin Harz, Jerusalem-Berlin-Vienna.

Idelsohn, A. Z., *Jewish Music in Its Historical Development,* Henry Holt & Co., 1929, New York.

Jackson, George Pullen, *America's Folkways,* in *Virginia Quarterly Review,* January 1936.

Jackson, George Pullen, *White Spirituals in the Southern Uplands,* The University of North Carolina Press, Chapel Hill, 1933.

BIBLIOGRAPHY

Jeanneret, A., *Le Negre et la Jazz*, in *Revue Musicale*, July 1927.

Johnson, James Weldon, *The Book of American Negro Spirituals*, The Viking Press, New York, 1925.

Johnson, James Weldon, *The Second Book of Negro Spirituals*, The Viking Press, New York, 1926.

Kallen, Horace Meyer, *Swing as Surrealist Music*, in *Art & Freedom*, New York, 1942, v. 2, p. 831.

Knowlton, Don, *The Anatomy of Jazz*, in *Harper's*, April, 1926.

Koebner, Franz Wolfgang, *Jazz und Shimmy*, Berlin, Dr. Eysler & Co., 1921.

Kool, Jaap, *The Triumph of the Jungle*, in *Littell's Living Age*, Feb. 1924, v. 324, p. 338.

Krehbiel, Henry Edward, *Afro-American Folk Songs*, G. Schirmer, New York, 1914.

Lake, Mayhew Lester, *The Wizard Trombone Jazzer*, G. Fischer, New York, 1919.

Lambert, Constant, *Jazz*, in *Life and Letters*, London, 1928, v. 1, p. 124.

Lambert, Constant, *Music Ho!*, Faber & Faber, Ltd., London, 1934.

Lange, Arthur, *Arranging for the Modern Dance Orchestra*, Robbins Music Corp., New York, 1927.

Lastrucci, Carlo L., *The Professional Dance Musician*, in *Journal of Musicology*, Greenfield, 1941, v. 3, p. 168.

Laubenstein, Paul Fritz, *Jazz, Debit and Credit*, in *Musical Quarterly*, October, 1929.

Lee, George Washington, *Beale Street, Where the Blues Began*, R. O. Ballou, New York, 1934.

Locke, Alain Le Roy, *The Negro and His Music*, The Associates in Negro Folk Education, Washington, D. C., 1936.

Lomax, Alan and John A., *Negro Folk Songs as Sung by Lead Belly, "king of the twelve string guitar players of the world," long time convict in the penitentiaries of Texas and Louisiana*, The Macmillan Co., New York, 1936.

Lomax, John and Alan, *American Ballads and Folk Songs*, Macmillan, New York, 1934.

JAZZ: HOT AND HYBRID

Marks, Edward Bennet, *They All Sang*, The Viking Press, New York, 1934.

Mason, Daniel Gregory, *The Jazz Invasion*, in *Behold America*, by Samuel Daniel Schmalhausen, Farrar & Rinehart, New York, 1933, p. 499.

Mayer-Serra, Otto, *Panorama de la Musica Mexicana Desde la Independencia Hasta la Actualidad*, El Colegio de Mexico, Mexico City, 1941.

Mendl, Robert William Sigismund, *The Appeal of Jazz*, P. Allan & Co., London, 1927.

Mila, Massimo, *Jazz Hot*, Milano, 1935.

Milhaud, Darius, *Etudes*, C. Aveline, Paris, 1927.

Miller, Glenn, *Glenn Miller's Method for Orchestral Arranging*, Mutual Music Society, Inc., New York, 1943.

Miller, Paul Eduard, *Yearbook of Swing*, Down Beat Publishing Co., Chicago, 1939.

Miller, Paul Eduard (Ed.), *Esquire's Jazz Book*, Smith & Durrell, Inc., New York, 1944.

Molitor, H., *La Musique chez les Negres*, in *Anthropos*, 1913, Bd. 8, p. 714.

Mongin, Stephane, *La Musique de Jazz*, in *Nouvelle Revue*, Paris, 1931, Ser. 4, Tome 113, p. 288.

Nelson, Stanley R., *All About Jazz*, Heath, Cranton, Ltd., London, 1934.

Niles, Abbe, *Jazz 1928: An Index Expurgatorius*, in *Bookman*, January 1929.

Ortmann, Otto Rudolph, *What Is Wrong with Modern Music?* in *American Mercury*, March 1930.

Osgood, Henry Osborne, *So This Is Jazz*, Little, Brown & Co., Boston, 1926.

Osgood, Henry Osborne, *The Anatomy of Jazz*, in *American Mercury*, New York, April 1926.

Panassie, Hugues, *Hot Jazz: The Guide to Swing Music*, M. Witmark & Sons, New York, 1936.

Panassie, Hugues, *The Real Jazz*, Smith & Durrell, New York, 1942.

BIBLIOGRAPHY

Pease, Sharon, *Boogie Woogie Piano Styles*, Forster Music Publisher, Inc., Chicago, 1940.

Ramsey, Frederic, *Jazzmen*, Harcourt, Brace & Co., New York, 1939.

Rottweiler, Hektor, *Ueber Jazz*, in *Zeitschrift für Sozialforschung*, Paris, 1936, Jahrg. 5, p. 235.

Saminsky, Lazare, *Music of the Ghetto and the Bible*, Bloch Publishing Co., New York, 1934.

Sargant, Norman and Tom, *Negro Music or the Origin of Jazz*, in *Musical Times*, London, 1931, v. 72, p. 653.

Sargeant, Winthrop, and Lahiri, Sarat, *A Study in East Indian Rhythm*, in *Musical Quarterly*, October 1931.

Sargeant, Winthrop, *Types of Quechua Melody*, in *Musical Quarterly*, April 1934.

Sargeant, Winthrop, article *Jazz*, in *International Cyclopedia of Music and Musicians*, Dodd, Mead & Co., New York, 1938.

Scully, Nora, *Native Tunes Collected in Basutoland*, in *Bantu Studies*, 1931, v. 5, p. 247.

Seldes, Gilbert, *The Seven Lively Arts*, Harper & Brothers, New York & London, 1924.

Smith, Charles Edward, *The Jazz Record Book*, Smith & Durell, New York, 1942.

Smith, Charles Edward, and Russell, William, *New Orleans Style*, in *Modern Music*, New York, 1941, v. 18, p. 235.

Sordillo, Fortunato, *Art of Jazzing for the Trombone*, O. Ditson & Co., Boston, 1920.

Specht, Paul L., *How They Become Name Bands*, Fine Arts Publications, New York, 1941.

Stringham, Edwin, *"Jazz," an Educational Problem*, in *Musical Quarterly*, April 1926.

Thomson, Virgil, *Jazz*, in *American Mercury*, New York, 1924, v. 2, p. 465.

Thomson, Virgil, *Swing Music*, in *Modern Music*, May–June, New York, 1936, p. 12.

JAZZ: HOT AND HYBRID

Tucker, A. N., *Primitive Tribal Music in the Southern Sudan at Social and Ceremonial Gatherings*, William Reeves Bookseller, Ltd., London.

Turner, W. J., *Music and Life*.

Turner, W. J., *Waltz Kings and Jazz Kings*, in *New Statesman*, April 17, 1926.

Vallee, Rudy, *Vagabond Dreams Come True*, E. P. Dutton & Co., New York, 1930.

Ward, W. E., *Music in the Gold Coast*, in *Gold Coast Review*, 1927, v. 3, p. 199.

Webb, H. Brook, *The Slang of Jazz*, in *American Speech*, New York, 1937, v. 12, p. 179.

Whiteman, Paul, *What Makes a Jazz Orchestra?* in *Musical Observer*, New York, August 1926, v. 25, p. 17.

Whiteman, Paul, and Lieber, Leslie, *How to Be a Bandleader*, Robert McBride, New York, 1941.

Whiteman, Paul, and McBride, Mary Margaret, *Jazz*, J. H. Sears & Co., Inc., New York, 1926.

Pleasants, Henry, *The Agony of Modern Music* Simon & Schuster, Inc., New York, 1955.

Jones, A.M., *Studies in African Music*, Oxford University Press, London, 1959.

INDEX

A

Adrian Rhythmic Trio, 233
Aesthetic aspects, 22, 28–44, 113, 212, 235–249
Aesthetic method of jazz, 254
Africa, musical, survey of, 261
African influence, 22, 40, 47, 52, 149–157, 214, 249
  recordings, 214
  tribal music, 48, 112, 214–220
African music, similarities to jazz, 263, 264
Afro-American Folksongs, 154, 161, 213
Afro-American music, 20–23, 48, 60, 64–67, 101, 115, 127–132, 154–156, 189, 191, 211–238
Agony of Modern Music, The, 253
Akst, Harry, 52
Alexander's Ragtime Band, 141
American Ballads and Folksongs, 248
American culture, jazz as exhibit of, 253
American Jazz Music, 222
American Negro, 25, 35–49, 128–146, 191, 214–220, 251, 252, 261, 264
  popular music, 52–55, 222
Americanization of jazz, 253
Amor Sincero, 121
Anacrusis, jazz, 95, 107–109
Anatomy of jazz, 59, 65–80, 221–230, 235–249
Anatomy of Jazz, The, 59
Anderson, Marian, 51
Anglo-Celtic ballads, 16, 52, 54, 112, 127, 133, 152, 192, 230
Antilles, music of, 124
Antoine, LeRoy, 123
Appoggiatura, 102
Arabian culture 34, 113
Argentine music, 118

Arkansas Traveler, 130
Armstrong, Louis "Satchmo," 18, 19, 49, 58, 93, 97, 99, 101, 159, 228, 251, 252, 253, 270
Arpeggios, rag piano, 133, 146, 157
Arranging, 23, 142–144, 231–240
Arranging for the Modern Dance Orchestra, 231, 246
Artistic integrity of hot jazz, 17, 113, 265-281
Aspasiu, Don, 121
Atonality, 255, 259, 260, 261
Audience participation, 25, 40, 48, 83, 231, 239
Auxiliary instruments, 231
Aymara Indians, 125
Aztec influence, 124–126

B

Babira rhythm, 216–219
Baby Face, 52, 53
Bach, Johann Sebastian, 33, 117
Balfe, 131
Ballanta-Taylor, Nicholas J. G., 41, 59, 99, 106, 113, 162, 192, 213, 217
Bandmasters, 221–234
Bands, 18–27, 39, 48, 58, 73, 82, 84, 87, 143, 159, 221–234, 261
Banjo, 144, 199, 222, 224–226
Bapere Circumcision Ritual, 215–219
Barber-shop harmony, 156, 177, 198-208, 274
Barn-dance tunes, 112, 129–131
"Baroque" ensemble, 255
Baroque-style jazz, 258
Barroom ditties, 16, 198
Basic rhythmic characteristics, 55–66, 214–220
Bathing Song, 123
Beale Street Mama, 171
Beaux Arts String Quartet, 259

290

INDEX

INDEX

INDEX

INDEX